The Wolds Way

by

David Rubinstein

Dalesman Books 1972

The Dalesman Publishing Company Ltd.,
Clapham (via Lancaster), Yorkshire.
First published 1972
© David Rubinstein 1972

ISBN: 0 85206 136 6

Printed and bound in Great Britain
FRETWELL & BRIAN LTD.
Silsden, Nr. Keighley, Yorkshire.

The Wolds Way

45p.

Contents

The cover picture of Wintringham church from Deep Dale Plantation is by Alan Marshall, and the title page photograph of a Wolds Way scene is by the Ramblers' Association. All uncredited photographs in the text are by George Kennedy. R. R. Dean prepared the maps.

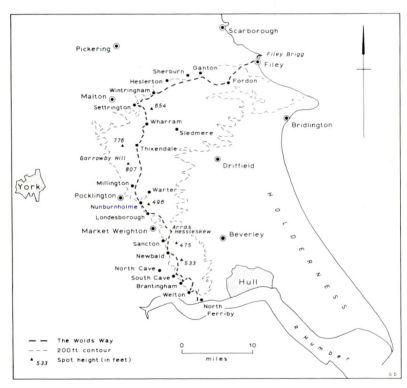

The Wolds Way.

Introduction

THE idea of a long-distance footpath across the Yorkshire Wolds is not new. A number of people have in fact walked their own version of the Wolds Way in past decades. Indeed, A. J. Brown actually used the term "The Wolds Way" in a rather different context forty years ago. (See chapter one below.) But the modern incarnation of the Wolds Way lies in a specific scheme put forward by the East Riding Area of the Ramblers' Association early in 1968. Rather to the Association's surprise, the idea immediately became extremely popular. The volume of public support has been enormous, extending to a letter from Canada to the East Riding County Council asking for a map of the route. Since 1968 there has been steady publicity for the Wolds Way, mainly but not only in Yorkshire. Articles, leaflets, radio and television appearances have served to keep the public informed and interested.

In July 1968 the East Riding County Council approved the Wolds Way "in principle," and in the following October the Countryside Commission, the Government body charged with responsibility for long-distance footpaths among many other concerns, also gave its approval in principle. For over two years the County Council's public rights of way staff surveyed possible routes and conducted negotiations, in particular with the Ramblers' Association, the National Farmers' Union and the Country Landowners' Association, as well as with individual landowners and occupiers. Eventually, in February 1971, the East Riding County Council approved a specific route for the Wolds Way, a route which is based on, but by no means identical to, the submissions of the Ramblers' Association. This route was sent to the Countryside Commission, to the Ramblers' Association and to the farming and landowning bodies for consideration. At the time of writing the negotiations for a mutually acceptable route are still taking place. The County Council's route is generally in excellent walking country, and it has been mainly followed here. In a few places

7

where a better route appears to be available, that has been followed instead.

Negotiations over the Wolds Way are complicated by the fact that footpaths and bridleways in the East Riding have until lately been in a sad plight. A recent calculation by the Ramblers' Association showed that in England and Wales as a whole there are two miles of foot and bridlepaths to every square mile. In the East Riding the figure is only one mile of path to every square mile. Much of the reason for this is the fact that, in the past, access to the countryside was not taken very seriously by the local authorities in the East Riding. When the Draft Map of Rights of Way for the county was published in 1953, nearly 500 paths were claimed by the Ramblers' Association and others as missing from the map. Due to unfortunate dilatoriness the claims were never heard. As a result of continued lack of progress, a unique legal procedure was adopted in the East Riding. The nearly 500 claims have still not been heard, and 683 objections by landowners and occupiers to paths on the Provisional Map (which was merely the reproduced Draft Map) were omitted from the next version, the so-called Definitive Map, published in 1968.

The result of this complicated legal situation is that, while other counties were preparing normal Definitive Maps, the East Riding map appeared without nearly 1200 foot and bridlepaths claimed as rights of way. This is a large proportion of the total number of rights of way, claimed or existing, in the East Riding. Since before 1968 there were very few footpaths signposts in the Riding, it is not surprising that the countryside was largely unknown except to experienced ramblers and to those who cheerfully ignored the law and went where they pleased—a situation which nobody can defend.

In the past few years, however, there have been marked improvements in the footpath situation. The East Riding County Council has not only been hard at work erecting signposts, but has also considered the status of many of the 1200 paths discussed above. In August, 1971, it published a Revised Draft Map, on which over 400 additional footpaths and bridleways appeared, and within the next few years the remainder of the 1200 will be considered and, hopefully, many of them added to the map. Although full opportunity exists for landowners and occupiers to object to paths on the Revised Draft Map, there is considerable evidence to support the claim that each of them is in fact a right of way. In the meantime, the status of the 1200 remains in suspended animation, claimed rights whose legal position remains to be determined.

Wolds Way country. Millington Pastures, looking east from Millington Dale.

The result for the 67 miles of the County Council's Wolds Way route will be evident. Only in certain sections, estimated as 18 miles, is the walker on definitive rights of way. For 16 miles he is on roads, mostly minor, some of them not made up. But 17 miles of the route follow paths whose status is legally undecided. In many of these cases there is no serious objection by landowners or occupiers, and virtually all of the disputed Wolds Way paths have been placed by the East Riding County Council on the Revised Draft Map recently published. But the legal resolution of their status remains for the future. Finally, along 16 miles of the Wolds Way no right of way is claimed to exist. As in the case of other long-distance footpaths, it was impossible to devise a through route entirely on existing or claimed rights of way. For example, the Cleveland Way in the North Riding, the continuation of the Wolds Way, consists of 93 miles, of which 14 are newly created rights of way, while 70 of the Pennine Way's 250 miles are new creations. In both cases many years of negotiations were needed before the legal formalities were completed. There has not yet been time for the legal creation of new rights of way along the Wolds Way, but in certain cases landowners have informally agreed to the creation of rights of way across their land. Where agreement has not yet been reached, mostly along the northern Wold escarpment, the route is not described here in detail. It is to be hoped that public support, which has been the driving force behind the Wolds Way to date, will sustain it through the remaining stages. It must be emphasised that the Wolds Way is a footpath, not a broad belt of access land. For much of its extent it follows heavily farmed land, and *it is essential that walkers keep to the path* and not stray onto farming land. Nor does the existence of a long-distance footpath, especially one whose legal formalities have not yet been completed, give any rights to campers.

Public transport is poor in the East Riding and may well get worse. However, at the time of writing it is possible to reach either end of the Wolds Way by train, and buses intersect the route at frequent points, though not at frequent intervals, so that with careful planning it should be possible for walkers to make day trips on the Way. For the person who wants to walk a longer stretch, there is a problem of accommodation. There is only one Youth Hostel on the Way, and that, at the nodal point of Thixendale, is open only on a part-time basis. But, as indicated in the text, there is a sufficient (but not abundant) number of places providing accommodation, mainly public houses, for the walker who *books in advance*. (Some of these places are at a little distance from the Wolds Way.) It is to be hoped that as the Way gains in popularity an increased number of private householders will be able to offer accommodation.

The Wolds Way can, of course, be walked in either direction. While making occasional suggestions to the walker starting from the south, I have chosen to describe its course from north to south. This is partly because the Way is very much part of the Two Ridings Walk, the continuation of the North Riding Cleveland Way. Since Bill Cowley's Dalesman book *The Cleveland Way* (1969) ends at Filey, I have started there and continued the route from north to south. Secondly, the southern end of the route is close to Hull, where many prospective Wolds Way walkers live. It seems logical to walk towards rather than away from home. Additionally, from North Ferriby, where the route ends, and from Hull, there is an excellent rail service to Selby, Doncaster and Leeds, and this will be useful to walkers from the west and south. So to those who object that the route described here is "backwards," I can only

10

ask indulgence and say that it must go in one direction or the other.

A word of caution is needed about the appearance of the countryside. Long-distance footpaths in mountain or moorland can be described in the confidence that their appearance will change little from season to season, year to year, with the obvious exception of snowfall. This is not the case with the Wolds Way. Changes in the seasons and changes in farming practice may make certain parts of the route difficult to recognise, as (for example) pasture falls under the plough or a field of corn becomes a root crop. I have tried to guard against this problem where possible, but the reader should also be on his guard for such cases.

Many people have helped to bring the Wolds Way into existence and assisted with the compilation of this book. I am grateful to the numerous friends who have walked parts of the route with me, and particularly to Donald Woodward, who has also read and criticised the text of the book. The staff of the Local History Library of the Hull Central Library have willingly provided much essential documentation. It is impossible to exaggerate the hard and vitally important work of the East Riding County Council, and especially of its public rights of way staff. However, it is fair to point out that the Wolds Way is the favourite child of the East Riding Area of the Ramblers' Association. Many of its members have given yeoman service over a lengthy period, in particular Jack Bower, Alan Dalton, Mike Hirst, Ray Hodge, Geoff Mell (who read and criticised an earlier version of this text), Ron Shaw and Stuart Wise. Colin Speakman of the West Riding Area of the Ramblers' Association and an experienced Dalesman writer has also given valued assistance. (Errors and inaccuracies which remain, however, are my sole responsibility.) The creation of the Wolds Way, a task still unfolding, has been the work of many hands. To dedicate this book to my friends and colleagues in the Ramblers' Association gives me much pleasure and pride.

DAVID RUBINSTEIN

August 1971.

1: *The Yorkshire Wolds*

THE Wolds are little known outside Yorkshire, perhaps even outside the East Riding. As Thomas Sheppard commented soon after the turn of the century in *Geological Rambles in East Yorkshire* (1902): "Having regard to their singular beauty, it is somewhat remarkable that the Yorkshire Wolds are not more generally known. Possibly the fact that the area contains no town of importance, whilst on the east are numerous watering-places, with their various attractions, and on the west is the grand old town of York, may to some extent account for this."

Other reasons for the general ignorance of the Yorkshire Wolds come to mind. The Wolds are in a sense a piece of southern England in the north. The northerner tends to think in terms of the North Yorkshire Moors, the Yorkshire Dales, the Peak and Lake Districts; moderate hills like the Wolds fail to impress him. Moreover, though the Wolds fall not far short of the highest points in southern England (Garrowby Hill top, at 807 feet, is the highest point on the Wolds; the highest point in Kent is 805 feet, in Sussex, 918 feet), the Wolds present less dramatic contrasts than the Downs of southern England. Their inclines are gentler and more gradual. Finally, for well over one hundred years the Wolds have been heavily cultivated; from being an expanse of rough sheep pasture dotted with rabbit warrens, they have become surprisingly fertile, and as a result there is little in the way of open dale and heath.

Yet no one with an open mind and not completely prejudiced against gentle hill country can fail to be impressed by the Wolds. Covering about 300 square miles, the Wolds contain about a quarter of the land expanse of the East Riding. Bernard Hobson, in *The East Riding of Yorkshire* (1924), a geographical-geological study of the Riding, points out that the Wolds form a crescent with its convex side turned west and north. Only on the northern edge, from Knapton nearly to the sea, do the Wolds form a continuous escarpment. On the western edges there are steep hills, while to the south and east the land gradually slopes down to the plain of Holderness

The Wolds contain few streams; the valleys are in the main dry. The reason for this is that being chalk they are porous, so that rain sinks through forming an underground reservoir which provides, among other things, water for Beverley and Hull. When the chalk is saturated by heavy rain the underground springs rise to the surface, notably in the case of the Gypsey Race which runs west from Bridlington. Many Wolds villages, especially in the north, are located where an impermeable layer of clay underlies the chalk, and water is thus easier to obtain; this explains the location of Staxton, Ganton, Sherburn, the Heslertons and Wintringham. Elsewhere on the Wolds, village and field ponds are an important source of water. Alan Harris, in his excellent study, *The Rural Landscape of the East Riding of Yorkshire, 1700-1850* (1961), points out that Woldsmen were particularly skilled at constructing cattle ponds, acquiring a reputation throughout Yorkshire for ponds of high quality, lined with puddled clay to prevent the water from escaping. The Wolds run west from the Filey-Bridlington area in a broad band for over 20 miles, to the west of Wintringham. Here they turn south, attaining in the area within reach of Thixendale their highest dimensions and some of their grandest views. As they move south the Wolds gradually narrow, until at the Humber their width is only about six miles.

During recorded history the population of the Wolds has always been small, in part because of the problem of obtaining water. With the coming of more intensive sheep farming in the fifteenth and early sixteenth centuries, many East Riding villages were deserted; there are as many as 100 "lost villages" in the East Riding, located particularly thickly on the Wolds. In one small area close to the Wolds Way, Wharram Percy (see chapter 3), Burdale, Towthorpe and Raisthorpe villages were all abandoned, and the Wolds Way also passes through the sites of deserted villages at the Camp, Cleaving and Wauldby. In the seventeenth and eighteenth centuries the Wolds were largely given over to sheep farming and rabbit warrens, though arable farming was carried on near farmsteads. As today, there was little woodland on the Wolds (although the Forestry Commission has recently been hard at work), Settrington woods being among the few old forests. Where the land is too steep for the plough, as in the area around Thixendale and, until the 1960s, in Millington Pastures, the layout of the grassy, rolling Wolds is probably similar now to that of 200 years ago. Travelling through Yorkshire in the 1720s Daniel Defoe commented: "I observed the middle of this riding or division of Yorkshire is very thin of towns, and consequently of people, being overspread with Woulds, that is to say, plains and downs, like those of Salisbury; on which they feed great numbers of sheep."

Enclosure came late, but it was complete. After about 1780, stimulated by Sir Christopher Sykes of Sledmere and other landowners, arable fields replaced the sheep-walks. New farmsteads were built, brick farms with red tiled roofs replacing the former structures of chalk and thatch. By 1850 permanent grassland was rare, and in 1869 a contemporary commented that the Wolds were "purely tillage" and "a large garden divided into beds." Although parts of the Wolds even today contain much pasture and unused scrub, as the Wolds Way walker will see, after 1850 the common fields and sheep-walks had largely gone. The fact that the district was so largely and suddenly transformed helps to explain why there are few ancient buildings on the Wolds, apart from some splendid churches and a few country houses. Renewal was the order of the day, and the older type of cottage was torn down and replaced.

There is abundant evidence of ancient settlement on the Wolds. Ancient dykes and earthworks abound, and the Wolds Way follows them in a number of places. (For an account of some of these, see the fascinating description of Bartindale Farm, Hunmanby, near the Wolds Way, in W. G. Hoskins, ed., *History from the Farm,* 1970.) Many long barrows from the New Stone Age have been found on or close to the Wolds, at Folkton, Willerby, Heslerton and Market Weighton among other places. Duggleby Howe is a splendid example of a round barrow of late New Stone Age date, while Iron Age remains have been found in many places. In June 1971, archaeologists working in the East Riding discovered the complete and undamaged remains of a chariot burial, the grave of a chieftain with his possessions. The chariot retains its two wheels, each with 12 spokes, bronze fittings and iron tyres. These finds at Garton-on-the-Wolds, near Driffield and about eight miles east of the Wolds Way, have been described by archaeologists as one of the greatest Iron Age discoveries made in Britain in this century. They are to be presented to Hull Museum.

The Garton discoveries, while dramatic, are not unique. Arras, near Market Weighton, was a centre of Iron Age settlement by the Parisi tribe, and many graves have been found there, containing bronze ornaments, chariots and other remains. The Romans were also much in evidence on the

14

Wolds, a number of finds having been made along the Wolds Way at Millington, Thixendale, North Newbald, Brantingham and (in the summer of 1971) Welton, to say nothing of the extensive villa remains discovered at Rudston, six or seven miles south of the Wolds Way and on the southern edge of the Wolds. A supposed Roman arena has been found at Hessleskew, near Sancton, and a Roman road ran from Malton to Brough (the Roman Petuaria), meeting the Wolds Way near Londesborough and Millington.

John George Hall, writing in 1892 (*A History of South Cave*), commented of the area around Sancton: "Almost every field in and around the parish is rich in relics of the Britons, Romans, and Saxons, who, in their turn, lived and died here." There were British food jars, Roman coins, and Saxon pottery. With a local guide, Hall went to a hill near Sancton, and after digging found an almost whole early British urn. Within a mile of Hessleskew, he commented, remains had been found from a lengthy period, dating from the time of the Romans to the first Elizabeth. Writing more recently, A. G. Dickens discovered "countless fragments" of Anglo-Saxon urns, "scattered over a ploughed field on Sancton Wold, and was rewarded for lingering by the usual soaking downpour which accompanies a casual archaeological ramble in the more shelterless expanses of East Yorkshire." (*The East Riding of Yorkshire with Hull and York,* 1954). Many archaeological finds from the Wolds may be seen at the Mortimer Archaeological Collection in the Hull Transport Museum.

The Wold country then, while making few claims to superlatives on grounds either of landscape or history, is full of interest. It is an area offering many different kinds of attraction, the scenery changing from hills to valleys to woodland. Because the Wolds are the only hills for many miles about, the views from their tops to the Vale of Pickering and the North York Moors, across the Vale of York to York Minster, and down to the Humber and north Lincolnshire, are often very fine. A. J. Brown, that great Yorkshire walker and writer (to whose books the following pages repeatedly indicate my debt), commented in *Broad Acres* (1948): "Truly it is in the Wolds that one derives perhaps the best impression of a land of broad acres; for from any of the gentle ridges one looks over immense vistas of undulating arable land, acres and acres of corn and of green pastures. This, one feels, is certainly Yorkshire at its richest and best."

In an earlier work, *Tramping in Yorkshire* (1932), Brown commented: "Let me go the Wolds Way without more ado."

He meant a general ramble rather than a linear path across the Wolds, but Brown's is the only account known to me of rambling in the Wolds, and this book tries to follow his pioneering footsteps. In *Tramping in Yorkshire,* Brown describes the Wolds in terms which are still relevant: "There is about the Wold country a quietness and benignity not elsewhere (I think) to be found in the shire. It is not the inviolate quietness of the northern hills; it is not the peace of the remoter dales, but rather a pastoral peace. The scattered villages that lie off the main roads seem to have escaped the tumult and the notice of the modern world; they are in the world but not of it; little communities of people living natural sheltered lives and taking small heed of the march of affairs beyond." It is this quiet, isolated and lovely world which is here described.

Archaeology on the Wolds Way. Walkers at Wharram Percy church.
(Author)

2: *Filey -West Heslerton*

THE Wolds Way begins on Filey Brigg, but there is a public right of way from the North Riding boundary, where the Cleveland Way long-distance footpath begins and ends. The North Riding coast south of Scarborough is scarred with caravans and other obtrusive holiday buildings, but the East Riding stretch from the county boundary to Filey is superb, with steep cliffs, the blue-green sea and contrasting green fields. The path, though of varying width, is easy to follow.

As you approach Filey, there is a magnificent view. In front is Filey Bay, with the steep chalk cliffs of Speeton and Bempton forming a striking landmark on the other side of the bay. Nearer at hand the vista is closed by Filey Brigg, a natural formation which instantly spells Filey to anyone who has seen it. The narrow headland with red clay walls going out to the Brigg proper is known as Carr Nase. At its end a Roman signal station once stood; today it is the site of a coastguard lookout point. Filey Brigg itself consists of a rocky outcrop extending into the sea. It is exhilarating to stand on the level stone platform of the Brigg, buffeted by wind and spray, enjoying the view extending to Scarborough Castle to the north and to Flamborough Head to the south. John Cole, in his *History and Antiquities of Filey* (1828), wrote of Filey Brigg in these terms: "Standing on these rocks what a glorious prospect! To the right what a magnificent bay! Sweeping round for miles till it terminates at Flamborough . . . To the left lies, stretching far away, a rocky shore, apparently resting on Scarborough hill, whose Castle proudly rises paramount over all: while on the hard, firm sands of Filey, numbers of well-dressed visitors remind one of the neighbourhood of civilized men." There is no doubt that Filey Bay, with the cliffs, the Brigg and the fishing cobles on the quay, is one of the finest bays on the east coast of England.[1]

1.   One can only view with horror the current plans for a caravan park and other obtrusive developments almost on Filey Brigg itself.

Filey town offers the usual facilities of a coastal resort. There are many places for the traveller to stay, to eat and drink, and trains to Hull and Scarborough. The railway service between Scarborough, Filey, Bridlington, Driffield, Beverley and Hull is paralleled by the East Yorkshire bus services 12 and (in part) 11. To the west there are two United buses on Thursdays and three on Saturdays (but none on other days) to Muston, Folkton, Flixton and Staxton (service 115). At Staxton you join the West Yorkshire company's Scarborough-York service 43, which (with service 84) operates daily buses at hourly or more frequent intervals via Ganton, Sherburn and West Heslerton, to Malton (railway connection) and York. The 43 bus runs on the main A64 road, parallel to the northern stretch of the Wolds Way. Thus you are never more than two or three miles from public transport along this stretch, and for much of it less than a mile away. (The stations on the Scarborough-Malton railway line have been closed between Seamer and Malton.)

Although Filey has less historical interest than some other coastal towns, there are some attractive old houses, especially in Queen Street. Two whitewashed, red-tiled cottages at the top of Queen Street, with a black and white inscription bearing the date 1696, a coat of arms and the words "The fear of God be in you", were renovated and opened as a folk museum and display centre in 1970. The exhibits relate to the sea, country customs and life in Filey, and are of considerable interest. Church Street, nearby, has more attractive houses, including one of red brick dated 1705. The parish church of St. Oswald has many interesting features. It is a mixture of Norman and Early English Gothic styles, to which considerable restoration has been made. There is a massive central tower, a fine Norman south door and an impressive nave arcade. Note the rough figure on the south aisle wall and the semi-circular memorial on a pillar at the north-east end of the nave dated 1750.

The coastline and Filey are no more than appetisers to the Wolds Way. You leave Filey by the Muston road (A 1039), turning right at the end of the town onto a cinder track shortly before a speed de-restriction sign and the Filey county secondary school. The track soon becomes a path; after about 200 yards you leave it to turn left by a stile and a bridge, following the edge of the school playing fields. The path climbs a hill, giving views of Scarborough and the monument on Oliver's Mount to the north. Keeping to the hedgerows you cross a stile and come to the Reighton-Gristhorpe road (A 165). On the other side of the road and slightly to the right is another

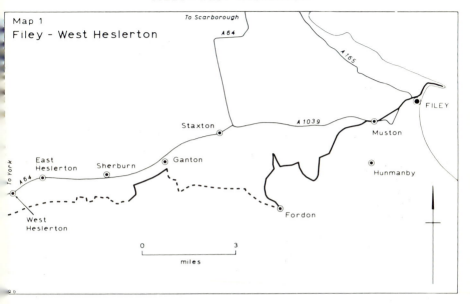

Map 1
Filey - West Heslerton

stile. You must now cross two low-lying fields in which the definitive right of way has been ploughed out. Make for the south side of a white bungalow, and emerge onto a little green at the eastern end of Muston village.

Muston has a nineteenth century church with a clock on its bellcote and a tree-lined walk, the *Ship Inn* with curved gables (no accommodation) and the striking eighteenth century Muston Hall, with willows and other fine trees in its lovely garden. There is a cafe and several places offering accommodation, notably a house bearing the initials RBE and the date 1755 (Mrs. Thistleton, Cross Keys House, no 'phone), and the Muston Lodge Guesthouse (tel. Filey 3258), a pleasant white building with black trimmings and the coat of arms of the Beswick family.

Shortly after the end of the straggling village, where the road bears right, turn left through a white gate and then to the right and up the hill, keeping on grassland and then to the left of the hedgerow. A track leads steadily uphill; turning round you have a magnificent view to the right of Bempton cliffs, standing sheer, above four hundred feet high. In the spring thousands of nesting birds may be seen along these cliffs. Muston village lies in the dip below and on the left is Scarborough Castle and a wide panorama of blue sea. The view is marred only by numerous caravans, especially in the vicinity of Reighton Gap.

At the top of the hill the route is barred by a hedgerow. Go through a gap in the hedge and straight across a ploughed field on a definitive right of way, then turning left join a farm track which emerges onto the Hunmanby-Folkton road opposite Stockingdale Farm. (If you are coming from the west, be careful not to descend the track to the main road, which comes out rather more than a mile west of Muston; leave the track and turn right by the second line of electricity wires.) Cross the road and keep the farm on your right as you follow the cart track. A hundred yards beyond the farm go through a gate and turn right, along a farm track immediately south of the wood called Long Plantation. The wood follows the line of an ancient earthwork. Descending into Stocking Dale turn sharply left, through the lovely wooded valley, the first of many Wold valleys to come. Follow the track along this secluded, sheltered route for about a mile. At its end the valley emerges into a wider setting at the Camp, the site of a deserted settlement. A few mounds and a round pond (Camp Well) are all that now remain, but in 1855 Robert Knox wrote that it was only about a hundred years since the spot was finally abandoned. "I noticed", he continued, "at this deserted village Camp, certain blue stones which had stood at the doors of the cottages (as at Bempton), and were used formerly to beat upon, instead of washing linen, garments, &c. when lotium or urine supplied the place of soap." (*Eastern Yorkshire*) Camp Dale leads off to the north-west. Walk on rough grass to a gate 200 yards ahead, and then cross a ploughed field (it is a definitive right of way), after which Camp Dale becomes a narrow valley with a clearly marked path. The route is characteristic Wold country—treeless hill slopes, attractive and lonely.

Shortly after passing another field pond and just before reaching a fence (beyond which the right of way leads to Folkton), turn to the left and up Raven Dale, following a cart track below the line of an earthwork. There are lovely views back into Camp Dale. After an uphill pull you come onto the Flixton-Fordon road—turn to the right along the road. From the top of the hill there are distant views of the North York Moors; less attractive are the towers of the RAF radar station at Staxton Wold to the left, and the Tilcon Flixton Quarry on the right of the road. After a little less than half a mile turn left into Lang Dale, reaching the dale end through a gate a

Filey Brigg. (A. L. Kemp; Crown Copyright reserved).

few feet from the road. For a short distance the route through the dale runs parallel to the road, then bears off to the right. Again the scenery is characterised by the treeless loneliness of the high Wolds. After about quarter of a mile there is an arable field to cross before you reach the pleasant valley of Nicker Pit extending to the left. There is now a good track running through the grassy Lang Dale. After another quarter of a mile the dale ends at a broader valley. A chalk farm road leads uphill on the left to North Fordon Farm, but you continue straight ahead on a clear path just above an arable field.

The mile along North Dale into the hamlet of Fordon is a charming route, the bare valleys broken by belts of trees. Towards the southern end an arable field can be avoided by keeping to the hill slope above it, and a little later the path becomes somewhat overgrown. Go through the farmyard of Low Fordon Farm, and out to the road by a telephone box. (There is no village shop or other amenity in the hamlet.) A. J. Brown wrote that Fordon was reputed to be the smallest

21

village in Yorkshire, "and", he added, "it is certainly one of
the most secluded . . . one of the most charming corners of the
Wold country." Fordon church is tiny and very attractive; like
the hamlet itself it claims to be the smallest in Yorkshire.
There is a pretty bellcote, a handsome tie-beamed roof and a
few Norman remains, including the font. The church is used
only once a year, for a Harvest Festival in early October, but
it is open to visitors and well worth visiting.

From Fordon for the ten miles to the West Heslerton-West
Lutton road, the Wolds Way consists mainly of paths along
which new rights of way must be created. As a result, and so
as not to prejudice the negotiations, the route will be described
in detail only west of Ganton where there is a claimed right of
way. From Fordon the intended route follows lonely Wold
valleys to Ganton. However, for the present it is advisable
to follow the road past High Fordon and Willerby Wold
Houses and along to Ganton Wold Farm. It is a reasonably
attractive road, hilly in places and little used by motor traffic.
There are extensive views, even though among them is the
obtrusive RAF Staxton station. A number of prehistoric sites
are in the area, but it is disappointing to find that the Willerby
Wold long barrow, a remarkable New Stone Age (2500-1700

Fordon, an outstandingly attractive point on the Wolds Way. Left: Walkers near Fordon. Above: Fordon village.

B.C.) crematorium which has yielded a number of finds, is now hardly more than a ripple in a field of corn. Although it is 133 feet long, the barrow does not exceed four feet in height.

At Ganton Wold Farm you join the Foxholes-Ganton road, which carries a good deal of traffic at summer weekends. The road descends steeply, a lovely tree-lined route. On the right in the valley below is Ganton Hall. Though the Hall, a Victorian businessman's redbrick mansion in debased French chateau style, is not one of Yorkshire's finest buildings, it is extremely attractive when seen from the Wolds to the south. The Wold valleys, the Vale of Pickering and the North York Moors form a grand backcloth. Past the first entrance to Ganton Hall on the right, turn left through a gate and along a pretty farm track, also lined with trees.

At this point you would do well to go into Ganton village and in particular visit the church, which in early spring is a beautiful sight, behind a carpet of snowdrops and crocuses with a rippling stream. The church, which has a fine spire, dates mainly from the fifteenth century. Its most notable

23

feature is the south porch, which has a richly ribbed roof, fine carvings and a door with ancient C-shaped hinges. Inside, on the north-west wall of the nave (but rather too high to read with ease) is a memorial tablet dated 1792 and dedicated to cne William Wilson, a ploughman who served a grateful master until his death on returning home from work at the age of 86. "He was", the tablet informs us, "an example of honesty, industry & sobriety." Refreshment and accommodation may be found in Ganton at the *Greyhound Inn* (tel. Sherburn 242). There is also a general store and a frequent bus service to Scarborough, Malton and York (West Yorkshire 43 and 84).

From this point until West Heslerton it is intended that the Wolds Way should leave the lonely, bare Wold valleys which it has largely followed previously, and follow the Wold escarpment, with long, sweeping views of the Vale of Pickering and the North York Moors. A taste of what is to come may be seen when you leave Ganton. Continue on the tree-lined track mentioned earlier; after another gate the track becomes somewhat overgrown. Views of the Vale of Pickering open out on the right, while three hundred feet above looms the Wold escarpment. Continue on the track, out to the road leading from the hamlet of Potter Brompton, which you reach just north of the local manor house, Dawney Lodge, Cross the road and go straight ahead through the farmyard of Manor Farm, continuing on the light, powdery soil of the cart-track. Keep next to the hedgerows and field boundaries, turning sharply left one field before the row of trees which indicates the Ganton-Sherburn parish boundary. After a gap a hedgerow appears, which leads uphill to the western corner of Brow Plantation. Behind you are fine views of the Vale of Pickering and the Moors. Enter the wood by a gate and follow the path uphill and to the right. Another gate leads onto the next stretch of the Wolds Way across the middle of an enormous ploughed field. It is more sensible to turn to the right, keeping between ploughed fields on an uncultivated strip which gradually narrows and before very long comes out onto the Sherburn-Foxholes road.

Turn right and follow the road for about a mile to Sherburn. The route passes a dammed stream in a valley and High Mill Farm (dated 1843 on a stone plaque), where there are the fine remains of a water mill, with some of its machinery still in place. Another plaque informs the reader that the mill was reconstructed in 1842. It is still used to produce animal feed by electric power. (For details, see K. J. Allison, *East Riding Water-Mills*, East Yorkshire Local History Society (EYLHS) Pamphlet no. 26, 1970). Sherburn will be a good place to stop for anyone who has walked from Filey. It is a sizeable village, with food and accommodation at two inns, the *Pigeon Pie* (tel. Sherburn 383) and the *East Riding* (tel. Sherburn 386). There are several shops and a church with a fine Norman chancel arch and an arcaded Norman font. As at Ganton, buses (West Yorkshire 43 and 84) for Scarborough and York stop at Sherburn.

Since the proposed Wolds Way route on grassland along the escarpment will have to consist mainly of newly created rights of way, there is something to be said for taking the bus along the frantically busy A 64 road for the three miles to West Heslerton. Alternatively, should you wish to walk, there is a continuous pavement on the north side of the road to West Heslerton. Thus, while unpleasant, this stretch is not actually dangerous. There are extensive views to the left and right of the Wolds and Moors. From East Heslerton church there is a definitive right of way known as the Priest's Trod which leads to Glebe Farm, from which a minor road leads to West Hesler-

Woods near Ganton.

ton, but the Trod has been ploughed out and badly obstructed. The broach spire of East Heslerton church is a striking landmark and is even more impressive from the Wolds. Although this is a nineteenth century church designed by G. E. Street, it is quite attractive, with a pleasing thirteenth century-style interior. West Heslerton lacks accommodation, but it is a pleasant village, with Heslerton Hall, a pretty little school and schoolhouse (now the village hall) dated 1850 with a Diamond Jubilee clock (1897) and, even more important, a friendly publican who will allow you to eat your sandwiches in the *Dawnay Arms.*

West Heslerton church is largely rebuilt and rather dull, but the monument on the south wall of the nave to the agricultural pioneer Sir Christopher Sykes of Sledmere (d. 1801) is worth seeing. The monument was erected by Sykes's daughter Decima Hester Beatrix Foulis, and describes his work in creating arable fields from sheepwalks. Sykes's work, the monument tells us, will be "co-existent with time itself, a memorial more pure and satisfactory than any of the greatest conquerors, inasmuch as his object and endeavours were to beautify, not to deface, the features of nature: to provide food for man's sustenance, rather than to sacrifice human life upon the shrine of victory and ambition." An unusual monument to have been erected during the Napoleonic wars. The chancel has a richly carved recess culminating in a splendid pointed arch, and in front of the altar are gravestones with handsome eighteenth century lettering.

3: West Heslerton - Thixendale

WALK steeply uphill for nearly a mile on the wooded West Heslerton-West Lutton road, which has a most attractive valley on the left. Shortly past a sharp bend in the road, turn right at a stile, walk diagonally up a grassy field, and at the east end of Abbey Plantation cross another stile. From the field there are extensive views over West Heslerton Brow to the Vale of Pickering and beyond. Past the second stile you must follow the edge of a ploughed field for about quarter of a mile. This is unrewarding work, and it is to be hoped that in the future the path can be diverted either into Abbey Plantation on your right, or onto the north side of the wood on grass land. At the end of the field and just south of Knapton Plantation you pass through a gate and continue uphill; the path is clearly marked between the wood and a field. To the north, in Knapton Plantation, is a hill known as Staple Howe. It was the site of an important late Bronze Age settlement, and numerous remains have been found. Before long the path joins a forest road coming from the right (if you are coming from the west, leave the road where it starts to descend and bear to the right onto the path), and about 200 yards later you leave this road, turning left through a gate and up the hill. This brings you out onto a farm track where you turn right, past West Farm. The track goes downhill, giving good views of the Vale of Pickering. The enormous maltings on the B1258 road beyond West Knapton is a particularly prominent landmark.

A little over quarter of a mile past West Farm turn left on a clearly defined earthwork with a grass path along the top. Here again you have views of the Vale of Pickering, and here the Wolds Way, which has followed an east-west course since leaving the sea, turns to the south, its direction until it reaches the Humber. The large Forestry Commission woodland ahead of you is Deep Dale Plantation. Enter it by a gate a short distance from its western edge and follow a forest track. The track turns left after about 50 yards, but you continue straight

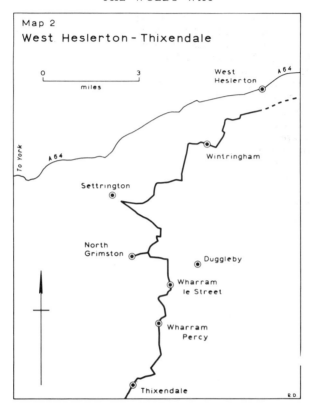

Map 2
West Heslerton - Thixendale

0   3
miles

West
Heslerton

A64

A64

To York

Wintringham

Settrington

North
Grimston

Duggleby

Wharram
le Street

Wharram
Percy

Thixendale

R.D.

ahead down the hill. In front is a spectacular view of the steep descent into Deep Dale with Wintringham church beyond, its high tower and spire framed in trees. This is one of the high points of the Wolds Way, literally as well as scenically, one of the most memorable but least visited views in Yorkshire.

Descending steeply between the trees you turn left at the chalk forestry road at the bottom of the hill. The road affords more good views of Wintringham church, since it keeps to a plateau above the fields along the edge of the woodland. Where the forestry road again turns sharply to the left follow it for one field width. At this point leave the road, go through a gate and follow the hedgerow past an old quarry which has become a rubbish tip, and so out to the road near Wintringham church. It is intended that Wintringham will be the first village through which the Wolds Way passes since leaving Muston, some

28

twenty miles earlier. It is a long village with many low, chalk-faced cottages and the estate of Place Newton at its east end. The estate gates, in classical style, are just off the main village road. Place Newton is a large, partly Georgian house. The grounds, which contain many beautiful, mature trees, are roughly grazed and not laid out as ornamental gardens.

Wintringham is dominated by its splendid fourteenth and fifteenth century church, built of pleasing yellow stone and impressive both inside and out. The steeple is imposing, and there are good Perpendicular windows, fine nave arches and a magnificent roof, gargoyles, a Norman font, a splendid south door with old iron hinges, medieval screens to the aisle chapels and a fine tiled floor, and some fifteenth century glass in the aisle windows. But the most interesting feature of Wintringham church is its numerous seventeenth and eighteenth century inscribed tablets. Two of them, beautifully lettered, contain the Lord's Prayer and the Creed, and the Ten Commandments. There is an acrostic on the name of John Lister (1608-1651), and a memorial to the churchwardens responsible for repairing the steeple in 1818. The most interesting of these tablets is nicely painted amid columns and scrolls on the south wall of the tower; dated 1723, it is an instruction to bellringers:

I pray you Gentlemen beware
And when you ring ye Bells take care;
For he that Rings and breaks a stay,
Must pay Sixpence without delay.
And if you ring in Spurs or Hatt
You must likewise pay Sixpence for that.
 (signed Michael Gill Clarke)

Evidently doggerel verse has an ancient lineage!

There is no public house in Wintringham and no accommodation, but there are pleasant trees and houses, in particular Manor House Farm, which has a lovely garden with a weeping willow. There are a number of somewhat surprising businesses for a small and remote village, including a builder and a motor-car showroom-cum-garage. There is also a post office with a well equipped shop. Three buses (Saturdays only) go to Malton, where there is a rail connection (West Yorkshire 95 and 95A). At Malton accommodation is available at the Youth Hostel on Derwent Bank (tel. Malton 2077) and at the Castle Hotel, 37 Castlegate (tel. Malton 2785). There are also pubs offering food and drink at Rillington, 2½ miles from Wintringham on the main A 64 road.

Leaving Wintringham the most desirable route is that leading from the east of the village down the narrow metalled road signposted to Home Farm. Continue down this road for about 150 yards, turning right at a gate just before the road turns to the left. Cross a grassy field, coming out at another gate. You are now on an unmetalled farm road, which leads south-west, giving fine views of the Wold escarpment, bare hill slopes crowned by woods. Behind you Wintringham church stands against the hilly woods of Deep Dale, and the Vale of Pickering stretches to the north. Then, after about a mile, the path turns to the west.

Although this route is a claimed right of way and appears on the Revised Draft Map, it is stoutly resisted by the landowner and occupier, and for the present the part of discretion is to avoid it. Instead, continue nearly to the west end of Wintringham. On the left is a low building looking like an old smithy. On the wall is a yellow circular plaque erected years ago by the Automobile Association, announcing that it is 4 miles to West Lutton, 7 to Malton and 221 to London. Past this building you turn left down a farm track, cross Wintringham Beck by a plank bridge and follow the track to the right. Cross the fields first on grassland, then hugging the hedgerows, emerging onto a farm road leading to Rowgate farm about half a mile from Wintringham.

The road is not much used, but it is metalled, and it is a longish drag for the mile up to Rowgate. Shortly before the farm, where the road turns to the right, continue straight ahead on a grass track. Go through a gate, past an old field pond and uphill, turning right at the end of a fence on a path leading north of an old chalkpit. The views behind you are extensive, including the Vale of Pickering, Wintringham and Deep Dale Plantation. Go through a gate and continue on the path, which for a short spell is undefined. It then becomes clear again and climbs Thorpe Bassett Brow, the ascent first gentle and then becoming steeper. At the top of the Brow you enter the pretty Many Thorns Plantation through a gate. Before doing so, have a last look at the beautiful views behind you.

The track climbs through the Plantation, more gently now, coming out at a gate to the deserted Many Thorns Farm. Enter the former farmyard by another gate, which leads onto the farm road. Leaving the farm buildings on your left you

Opposite: Church scenes on the Wolds Way. Top: Settrington church. Bottom: Norman font at North Grimston church.

have now three ploughed fields to cross, ploughed even though they are definitive public rights of way. (Almost without exception where the Wolds Way crosses ploughed fields it is on definitive rights of way, which are required by law—if not always in practice—to be restored after ploughing.) Eventually you reach the Settrington-Luttons road opposite Wold House Farm, called Wold Farm on the one-inch map. In April the track to the farm is lined with daffodils. There is a magnificent view across the Wolds to the south.

Take the track, going through the gate on your right next to a small corrugated building just before reaching the farm. You descend the hill into a charming green valley, and then climb the hill which leads to Wardale Farm. Don't go as far as the farm, but follow the path to the left over the brow of the hill. This broad, wooded valley, typical of the scenery around Settrington and North Grimston, is rather more like a southern valley complex than like the steep, bare Wolds. The route continues to the Settrington-Thorpe Bassett road, but it is difficult to follow and involves crossing several fences. It is accordingly wiser to reach the road by means of the short farm road serving Wardale Farm.

Turn left and continue down the road for about quarter of a mile, then left again through a gate and down a chalk farm track just east of a copse. However, most walkers will want to visit Settrington, less than half a mile further down the hill. Settrington is perhaps the prettiest village on the route of the Wolds Way. Built as an estate village, it has trim cottages with long gardens, a house with high brick walls which was formerly the rectory and is now known as Glebe House, another fine house called Greystones, a former water mill dated 1790 and Settrington Beck running through the middle of the village. There is again no public house (One is so often reminded on the Wolds of A. J. Brown's lamentation over Bainton, a village further south: "I must confess to a little disappointment when I found that Bainton did not possess an inn. The church is certainly full of interest, but after all a man needs a drink now and then."), but food and drink are available at the village shop, which is an off-licence. Occasional buses (East York-shire 34, 34A, 34B, none on Monday or Wednesday) go to Malton and Driffield; the service is quite good on Saturdays.

The outstanding feature of Settrington village is its magni-ficent eighteenth century great house, flanked by its (mainly) fifteenth century church. There is a beautiful lawn in front of the house and handsome grounds to the side, a summer house hidden in trees and a lake across the road. Though comparative-

The Wolds Way near Settrington. Left: Walkers above Rowgate Farm. Right: View towards North Grimston from Settrington Wood House Farm. (Author).

ly small, Settrington House is a splendid example of the English classical style and is beautifully maintained. It consists of a main block of seven bays in yellow stone, and two lower wings with fine round arched windows. Settrington church, while not so fine as Wintringham, is full of interest. Its best feature is its west tower with stepped buttresses. There is a thirteenth century south door and a number of interesting monuments and memorials dating from the seventeenth century. There is also a memorial to Isaac Taylor (1829-1901), a philologist and a prolific writer, who was rector of Settrington from 1875 until his death. Although not large, the church is painted white and is bright and attractive.

Returning to the Wolds Way, there is a continuous track from Settrington to North Grimston, about three miles away. The farm track leads to Low Bellmanear Farm, where you have another view of the valley earlier seen from Wold House and Wardale Farms. Keep Low Bellmanear on your left and continue on the track which leads into Settrington Wood. The chalk track, which goes steeply uphill, ends in the wood and becomes a still definable grass track. At the top of the hill you join a stony farm road. From this point there are splendid views back to Settrington House, the Vale of Pickering and the North York Moors. Turn right, and almost at once the track joins a second, leading down to the right to the keeper's

33

lodge. Do not take this track, but continue round to the left, pretty valleys opening out before you. The track reaches Settrington Wood House Farm, attractively situated on a plateau, where the track turns first to the right, then sharply to the left. From Wood House is a fine view of the hills of Cow Cliff and Grimston Brow. The valley land in front is green and lush, with grazing sheep—it is a charming scene.

Follow along the farm road, which is metalled near its western end, to North Grimston. It passes through pretty country, coming out at the Malton-Beverley road (B 1248). The *Queen's Head* public house is just to the right, and here food and drink and, for the first time since Sherburn, bed and breakfast are available (tel. North Grimston 255). You can also find occasional buses to the railway stations at Driffield and Malton (East Yorkshire 34, 34A, 34B). It should be noted that the only refreshment in Grimston is at the *Queen's Head*, since the post office lacks a shop. The only building worth examining apart from the pub is the church, which is of considerable interest. (There is also an attractive old vicarage sheltered by trees.) The thirteenth century tower has some interesting carvings, and there are good monuments and coffin lids in the chancel. The best part of the church is Norman, including the south door, a very fine chancel arch and the massive, round font, which is perhaps the most remarkable in the East Riding. It is decorated with scenes of the Last Supper and of Christ descending from the cross; the carving is characteristically crude and buoyant.

It is an unfortunate fact that south of North Grimston the potential route of the Wolds Way passes through exceptionally lovely country belonging to a landowner who, at the time of writing, is determined to oppose public footpaths across his land. The very attractive route to Wharram Grange Farm and down to the former Malton-Driffield railway line can accordingly not be recommended at this stage, and in fact all the footpaths recommended below between Wharram le Street and North Plantation, although placed by the East Riding County Council on the Revised Draft Map, are at present subject to the landowner's opposition.

Retrace your footsteps for about half a mile down the farm road leading to Settrington Wood House Farm. Shortly to the east of a gate and just before a bend in the road are two distinct hills on the south, with vehicle marks on the grass between them. Ascend between the hills to the road, the track becoming clearer as you go. Gain the road through a gate, just to the east of Grimston Hill House Farm. The road is Duggleby

High Street (B 1253), a very busy road, so exercise due care. There are wide grass verges, but the grass is long and not easy to walk through. You walk for over half a mile on this road, steeply uphill. To the left there are fine views of the Vale of Pickering and the North York Moors. A little past the top of the hill and an Observer Corps look-out, an earth and stone farm track crosses the road. Wharram le Street is clearly visible nearly a mile to the south, and you walk down the farm track to the village. (Duggleby, about a mile further on, has a post office and a shop; there are occasional buses, East Yorkshire 34, 34A, 34B. The sprawling village has a disused chapel but no church. A short distance to the south-east, just off the Sledmere road (B 1253), is Duggleby Howe, a striking landmark which was excavated in 1890; many human bones, flint axes and other tools were found. Dating from between 2100 and 1700 B.C. Duggleby Howe is one of the largest round barrows in Great Britain. It is 120 feet in diameter and about 20 feet high, but originally it was at least ten feet higher.)

You join the main Malton-Beverley road (B 1248) just south of the sign bearing the words Wharram le Street at the north end of the village. Although the road is busy, there is a pavement on its west side. (Coming from the south, turn right onto the farm road just before the sign.) Wharram le Street is more a collection of farms than a village, and some of the farmhouses are quite attractive. There is a post office with a small shop attached, a telephone, and the 34, 34A and 34B buses to Malton and Driffield. The old school, now the village hall, is dated 1871. The church, whose yard has views of the Vale of Pickering and the Moors, has an interesting Saxon or early Norman tower with high windows and a west door; it also has a Norman south door.

From the crossroads at Wharram le Street, walk down the road signposted to Birdsall. It leads at the bottom of a hill to the former Wharram station of the old Malton-Driffield railway. The line, which passes through very attractive country, has an interesting history, a little of which is worth telling. Building the line, which was opened in 1853, was a considerable engineering triumph, involving not only fairly steep gradients but, from Burdale to North Grimston, extensive engineering work. When the line was opened the *Eastern Counties Herald* wrote (26 May 1853) of this stretch: "The line is a constant succession of embankments, bridges and viaducts, and here all the skill of the engineer, A. L. Dickens, Esq., has been called into play. The very treacherous character of the clay has caused infinite trouble. Thousands upon thousands of tons of rock have been sunk to obtain a secure foundation." Burdale Tunnel, less than a mile to the south and about a mile long, took nearly six years to build. The *Herald* commented that "the singular encampment for the accommodation of the workmen, on the top of the hill, has become a familiar object in the topography of the district." (It is perhaps not surprising that the line cost about £10,000 per mile to build.) But although the *Herald* paid tribute to the "general orderly and good behaviour" of the railway navvies, this was not the whole story. In 1848 during a period of financial crisis work on the Burdale Tunnel was stopped, and early in 1849 fifty discharged workmen ran riot, among other misdemeanours "killing game and whatever came their way," as the *Yorkshire Gazette* wrote on 6 January 1849. The line was a godsend to the Wolds farmers, especially during the winter, and also took stone from the quarries at Burdale and Wharram. In 1925 Wharram traffic alone amounted to over 100,000 tons of chalk. The line closed to passenger traffic in 1950, to goods in 1958.

It is a far cry from the formerly busy Wharram quarry and an even farther cry from the boisterous navvies of the 1840s to the quiet, disused line of today. Although the claimed right of way appears on the Revised Draft Map and has been used for many years (Indeed, the Arthur Mee guide to the East Riding of 1964 tells the visitor to approach Wharram Percy "along the road to the (now disused) railway station, and then along the path alongside the railway line near the old quarry"), it is opposed by the local landowner. Turn left at the entrance to the former Wharram station, past a sign reading "No Entry Private Road". The old line is now a gravel track. On your left are buildings of the disused Wharram quarry (the quarry itself is now a nature reserve), including disused kilns and a large concrete structure used as a barn; the view is prettier to the right. The claimed right of way is just to the left (east) of the former line, but in places it is difficult to find. Since the path is overgrown and the quarry is a nature reserve, it is to be hoped that the owners of the former line will agree to the path being diverted onto the line for this short stretch.

A little over half a mile from Wharram station you reach a farm road, which crosses the railway on a bridge, going uphill to the left to Bella House Farm and the main North Grimston-Beverley road. It is here that you meet a possible diversion of the Wolds Way route. This involves continuing south on the main B 1248 road for nearly half a mile from Wharram crossroads, to the road signposted "Burdale 2" and also Bella Farm. Keep to the west side of the road where there

36

is a wide grass verge and no hedgerow. The Burdale road is metalled, but is not in good condition and is little used by motorists. Continue down this road for about two-thirds of a mile, past Bella Farm. About 200 yards past the farm, just before a hedgerow, a chalk track leads south down the hill. Follow the track, cross the gate by a stile and the old railway line on the bridge mentioned earlier. It is hardly necessary to point out that this is a much inferior means of reaching Wharram Percy to the route previously described. From the railway bridge (just below which is the north entrance to Burdale Tunnel) turn to the right, where the track takes you up to the famous ruined village of Wharram Percy. Keep to the left fork where it divides just before the cottages, which you keep immediately on your left (the landowner has agreed this route).

Wharram Percy has been described by the leading expert in the field, Maurice Beresford, as "of all village sites so far excavated in England . . . the most promising." (*The Lost Villages of England*, 1954). The village was abandoned, not after the Black Death in the fourteenth century, but about the year 1500, when sheep replaced arable fields. It was one of four villages deserted in the same area, the others being Burdale, Raisthorpe and Towthorpe. However, Wharram church served Thixendale village until the later nineteenth century when Thixendale acquired its own church, and as a result occasional services went on at Wharram as late as 1939. The local landowners several times repaired the church, but part of the tower fell in 1960. The building which now remains dates from Norman times to the fifteenth century, and recently an early Saxon church has been uncovered underneath it. At present the church ruins are being preserved, and an interesting early script has been revealed on the north wall of the nave.

Excavations have been taking place at Wharram Percy for about twenty years. The remains of the village are on the hill slope west of the church, and among the discoveries are the foundations of a twelfth century manor house and the houses of peasants. (An excellent source to begin a study of Wharram Percy is K. J. Allison's *Deserted Villages,* 1970. Better yet join one of the digs held annually in July.) At present the remains uncovered each summer are covered up again until the next year, but before long Wharram Percy will come under the guardianship of the Department of the Environment (the former Ministry of Public Buildings and Works) and its remains will be open to the public.

Leaving Wharram Percy church behind you, go through a

gate and turn left, crossing the beck where stones have been laid to ease a passage. Here turn diagonally to the left, uphill on a clear path across the grassy slope. At the top of the hill walk along the path, which is distinct and easy to follow, through tall grass with a cornfield on your left. The next stretch of about three-quarters of a mile is superb walking country. Wharram Percy church and the Vale of Pickering are behind you. Opposite, beyond a corn field, is the deep green of Wharram Percy Plantation, and ahead is North Plantation. The whole area is undisturbed; civilisation seems far, far away. As you continue, the splendid valley of Deep Dale opens below you on the right, the Wold wall curving smoothly, almost as if it were man-made. At nearly 700 feet you are at one of the highest points of the Wolds Way. Note how Deep Dale sweeps away to the right, before ending as a ripple in a hill slope below Wharram Percy House. At the end of this stretch, in front of North Plantation, you meet a famous old right of way leading west towards Aldro and east to the Malton-Beverley road. About half a mile east of where you are now standing is the line of the Burdale Tunnel, and an air shaft from the tunnel can be seen on the right in a field. It is a delightful spot, unspoiled by pylons or any other obtrusive evidence of man. It was of this track that A. J. Brown wrote in 1932 in words still entirely appropriate: "This is the sort of track I would rather follow than all the metalled roads constructed of man . . . It is remote from the world of men and takes one over the ridge of the escarpment . . .The earth is so full of chalky flint hereabouts that a new ploughed field looks as if it has been sprinkled with cherry-blossom or snowflakes. The land falls away to the left and right but the track clings to the ridge and rewards one with glorious views. They talk about walking on top of the world; but walking on top of the Wold is good enough for me on such a morning and such a track."

Where you are standing, above Deep Dale with splendid views back to Wharram Percy and the Vale of Pickering, there is a gate on your left. Go through this gate and another on your right, straight ahead on a grass path for 50 yards, then bear right through long grass. Cross the little fence and turn to the left, walking on meadow land on whch sheep graze, with the narrow tongue of North Plantation immediately to your left. Before long you begin to descend, the views opening out to the south. Continue across the meadow until you reach a farm road, where you turn to the right. As you continue downhill, there are lovely views of the valley and the Wolds opposite Raisthorpe. The track continues to descend to Raisthorpe

Farm. As you descend, notice the former chalkpit on the hill opposite, finely shaped in scallop form. (Coming from the south, be sure to take the track to the right after leaving Raisthorpe, not the track which goes straight ahead to the now disused Wold House Farm).

At Raisthorpe, the site of another deserted village, the claimed right of way (which appears on the Revised Draft Map) has received rough treatment, a barn having been built across it, fences erected and crops sown. It is to be hoped that a route for the right of way will be established, but for the present it is the part of discretion to continue past the farm to the Thixendale-Burdale road. (Note the typical Wold farmpond as you pass Raisthorpe.) Remain on the road for about half a mile until you reach the parish boundary north-east of Thixendale, immediately before a large ash which spreads across the road. At the parish boundary the path becomes distinct, only about fifty yards to the right of the road. The bare Wolds rear up on all sides, fringed with trees, in lovely contrast to the views which you have had from the hilltops. The path passes football and cricket pitches, and the first building which you reach in Thixendale village is the *Cross Keys Inn* (no accommodation), a suitable place to end a long walk.

Thixendale, though lacking outstanding buildings, is superbly situated. (It is very isolated; there is no bus service to the village.) In the centre of a complicated dry-valley network—A. J. Brown names its sixteen dales as Waterdale (which carries the Thixendale-Leavening road), Williedale, Brubberdale, Courtdale, Honeydale, Buckdale, Longdale, Middledale, Breckondale, Warrendale, Broadholmedale, Pluckhamdale, Millamdale, Fotherdale, Bowdale and Fairydale—it has as nice a situation as any village in the Wolds. But Thixendale must pay the price, for it is often badly snowed up in winter. The enterprising villagers have raised £500 and purchased the old school to use as a village hall. This was completed in 1970, and in the spring of 1971 the hall opened for the first time as a part-time Youth Hostel, the only hostel, it should be noted, in the East Riding. The plan is to use the building as a hostel during Easter and Spring Bank Holiday weeks, during the whole of July and August, and on all other weekends between Easter and the end of September. To date the hostel has more than met expectations, over 200 people having stayed in it by mid-August, 1971, including Swedes, Swiss and Australians[1]. The warden is the Thixendale village shopkeeper, Mr. L. Lyus,

1. The total for the 1971 season was 280.

Littlegarth, Thixendale (tel. Huggate 255).

Other accomodation in Thixendale is to be found in two cottages next to the pub. The owners are Mrs. S. Anstey, Round the Bend Cottage (tel. Huggate 237), and Mrs. R. Hall, Mayview Cottage (telephone via Mrs. Anstey). Teas are available at the quaint cottage of Miss Mary Stewart, next to the Youth Hostel. Thixendale church was provided in 1870 by Sir Tatton Sykes of Sledmere, the patron of much church building in the East Riding. The church, which has a bellcote in place of a tower, is an unassumingly pleasant neo-Gothic building. A notable attraction of Thixendale is the beautiful elm which has been preserved in the road in front of the old vicarage and adds character to the whole village.

Thixendale Youth Hostel. (Author)

4: *Thixendale - Arras*

LEAVE Thixendale by the Fridaythorpe road at the T junction. A hundred yards later is another junction where four roads meet. All the others branch off to the left, down the various valleys which meet at the village, but you keep straight on down the road signposted to Painsthorpe. Again you are in a lovely, lonely Wold valley, whose bare slopes are fringed with trees. There are nice views behind of Thixendale and the surrounding hills.After about half a mile the road curves to the right. There is a sign for a cattle grid and animals crossing, and at this point a cart-track leads left between two arable fields. Follow the track down the pretty valley, the hills and valleys sweeping round on all sides.

The route of the Wolds Way follows the valley bottom for about two miles before reaching the York-Driffield-Bridlington road. For about half the way you have a clear track to follow, but the route becomes rough towards the southern end. Look out for two possible difficulties about the half-way point. Coming from the south be sure not to take the track off to the right leading uphill to Gill's Farm. Walkers from the north must avoid going down Bradeham Dale, which (I write from grim experience, having misled a party of 16) will lead you out to the main road at Wayrham Farm, a mile to the west of where you should be, or at Fordham Farm, even further west. To avoid this error, when you reach the double fence turn sharply to the left, not straight ahead into Bradeham Dale. A little later you come to another apparent junction of valleys, but in fact the left-hand valley path soon ends at a hill side. Follow the right fork, walking in long grass, and where the valley again divides, turn right into the wooded Pluckham Dale. Near the southern end it is advisable to stay on the hill slope to the west of the wood called Pluckham Plantation, for the path through the plantation is badly overgrown. But do not dwell too much either on possible errors or on the under-growth. The whole of this valley stretch from Thixendale is quiet and peaceful, the hills beautifully proportioned, with just

enough trees to enhance the scene. It is one of the most attractive and unspoiled parts of the Wolds Way. However, walkers
are warned that one weekend in the early summer a motor-
cross rally is held towards the Thixendale end, rendering the
scene noisy and unpleasant.

At the southern end of this stretch follow the hedgerow
between the ploughed fields and out onto the main York-
Driffield-Bridlington road (A 166). Here you are only a couple
of miles east of Garrowby Hill, at 807 feet the highest point in
the East Riding. There are two buses a day (East Yorkshire
45) to Driffield, Bridlington and York. The road is very busy,
particularly with weekend coastal traffic, so cross with due
care. It is hoped that from this point a new right of way will be
dedicated across the ploughed field on Wold Farm. When
agreed, the Way will enter the field by two distinctive white
concrete blocks which resemble Roman milestones. Blocks of
this type distinguish the different fields (although many of the
hedgerows separating the fields no longer exist) of Wold Farm,
forming a distinctive feature which has aroused comment from
large numbers of passers-by in the decade or so since they were
erected. The blocks bear different inscriptions, the two at this
point reading "vallus" and "vallis."

The plan is to keep the hedgerows on your immediate
right across the field, passing a small pond in the middle and
emerging from the field by more "milestones," reading "alio"
and "Huggate aditus." You will then be on a minor road
leading to Huggate. Turn left here and follow the road for
about half a mile, past (East) Greenwick Farm with its distinctive barn on your right. At the second lot of "Roman milestones" on your left (reading "vallis watermanhole magna"
and "vallis watermanhole lingua") and a road junction, turn
right, following a track into Forestry Commission land.
(If you are coming from the south, turn left along the road
signposted to Stamford Bridge and York.) Until recently it was
thought that the farmer at Wold Farm had agreed to this
newly created right of way. The position is now in some doubt,
though it is to be hoped that before long this vitally important
short link will be definitely agreed. For the present, however,
it is necessary to ask permission of the farmer (who also
manages the petrol station at the corner of the Thixendale-
Huggate road where it crosses the A 166), or, exercising due
care, to walk along the A 166 for about half a mile and then
south to the Forestry Commission track by the Huggate road.

Shortly after beginning to descend the Forestry Commission
road into Greenwick Dale, you come to a gate bearing a

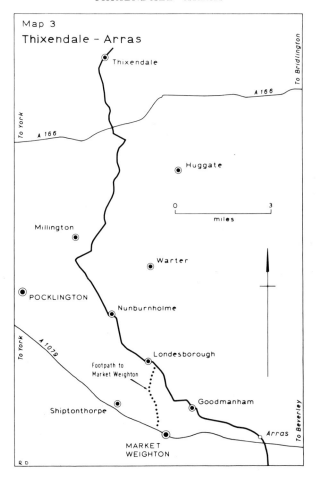

Map 3
Thixendale – Arras

Commission sign forbidding unauthorised vehicles. The path
levels out, swinging first to the left and then to the right, round
a steep valley slope. It then descends more sharply through the
trees. At the bottom of the hill you come out through a gate
and turn left. If you are coming from the south, be sure to turn
to the right here; do *not* follow the track round to the left. The
grassy track now goes to the south, past a somewhat dismal-
looking Forestry Commission plantation. Follow this clear
track along Tun Dale and Frendal Dale to the Millington-

Huggate road, a little over a mile away. This is again fine walking country, in typical Wold terrain; gradually the hills close in and grow higher. It was near the Millington end of this track, in a fine natural amphitheatre, that 250 Wolds Way ramblers gathered in October 1968 to hear a speech by Tom Stephenson, president of the Ramblers' Association and originator of the Pennine Way.

You come out onto the road through a gate. Cross the road and ascend the hill opposite; this involves crossing a fence. Follow the earthwork and a line of trees, keeping the trees to your left. It is a steep uphill pull, but it is well worth the effort, for from the ridged top of the earthwork there is a sweeping view of Millington Pastures and the surrounding countryside. Millington Pastures were long a survival of traditional Wold open pasture farming (A. J. Brown called them "a green paradise".) and a popular spot for family outings, and there was an outcry when they were enclosed and sown with crops in the early 1960s. The outcry reached its culmination with a protest ramble in November 1965, which failed in its main object. Two adjacent bridleways, however, were saved, leading across the Pastures to Millington Heights, a pretty route. Large numbers of visitors still gather in Millington Dale at weekends, and the site is ideal for creation as a Country Park. One of the bridleways follows the site of an old Roman road, and near this point were found in 1745 Roman buildings, mosaic pavements and coins.

Descend the hill, still on the earthwork. (N.B. If you want to avoid the sharp up-and-down, walk on the road to the south-west when emerging from Frendal Dale. Turn left after a few hundred yards at the signpost labelled "Public Bridleway Huggate 2," a somewhat inadequate notice in view of the fence across the route not far from the road. Whichever way you have reached this point, you now ascend the earthwork to the south-west. Here a chalk road has been made along the line of the earthwork, a pronounced gash across the face of the countryside. Ascend this steep hill, with its view of Millington Dale and Pastures and the Vale of York opening out in front. At the top of the hill keep to the track next to the fence. The track continues along the earthwork and becomes a path.

Opposite: Wooded country.   Top: A walker south of Thixendale. (Author).
Bottom: Greenwick Dale, near Millington.

Keep to this path for a little over half a mile; before you descend there are more fine views and a good spot for lunch or a rest. Down the valley to the right is the village of Millington; in front, a dark coniferous plantation and above it Warren Farm.

Cross the fence on your left and descend the hill, a very steep drop to the valley bottom. (Coming from the south, ascend the hill before you reach the fence, for the ascent on the far side of the fence is even steeper.) Along the valley bottom once ran a Roman road, a section of the Malton-Brough road. Turn left here along an ill-defined path until, in less than quarter of a mile, you reach a prominent gravel-filled gully ascending the hill steeply to the south-west. The earthwork continues along the top of the gully and this brings you to a gate at the top of the hill.

Go through the gate and along the earthwork, keeping the ploughed field on your right. There are fine views on the right of the Vale of York and closer at hand of the two bridleways across Millington Pastures. As you continue the Vale opens out, villages and fields spreading before you. Continue along the field edges until you reach a farm road just before Warren Farm. Turn right onto this road and then to the left, keeping

Left: A gathering of walkers. Ramblers' Association members are addressed by their president, Mr. Tom Stephenson, near Millington in 1968. (Cedric Emerson). Above: A lone walker. The author at the "Roman" farm near Huggate. (Peter Jackson).

the farm buildings to your right. If you wish to leave the Wolds Way here, a public right of way passes to the right of the farm and down to Millington, less than a mile away. Millington is nicely situated in the valley below the Wold escarpment; its small church has a good Norman south doorway, and if you book in advance, Mr. and Mrs. Holland at the charming *Gate Inn* (tel. Pocklington 2045) will give you dinner, bed and breakfast. A. J. Brown referred to the *Gate Inn* in 1932 as "a snug little place", and it still deserves that description. It is sad to relate that we are now in the kind of "dry" country which Brown deplored as much as we do; there is, unhappily, no public house directly on the Wolds Way between Thixendale and Goodmanham, a fearfully long stretch. So the *Gate Inn* is worth remembering. Two buses on Saturdays only will take you from Millington to Pocklington (East Yorkshire 93).

From the top of the escarpment is a fine view of Millington in the valley, with many hedgerowed fields before it; in the distance the Vale of York stretches away. Go through the farm gate and keep on the earthwork, which is at the top of the escarpment. A path is faintly marked on the ground; on your right the land falls away sharply. Continue across a fence and the path becomes clearer; rabbits race on the hill slopes before you. When you come to another fence turn sharply to the left, along the boundary between two fields; keep the boundary fence to your left. After about 200 yards turn to the right, and head across a field to the north-east edge of Warrendale Plantation. When you reach the plantation turn to the right on a grass track, walking along the edge of the pretty, hilly woodland. Descend the track, which offers fine views of the Vale of York, and, on clear days, York Minster. You soon reach a metalled road which runs between the nicely situated Rose Cottage to your right and (Low) Warrendale House (Farm) to your left. Here you turn left on a pretty access road to Warrendale.

Go round the farm, keeping the buildings on your right, then follow the cart-track, keeping the fence to your left. At the end of the field the track bears right, then left, and follows the line of the telegraph poles. Go through a gate and on grass land to the north-east edge of a wood. From this point turn diagonally to your left and uphill to a gate which opens onto the B1246 road. Before turning up to the road notice the fine views on the right of the eighteenth century Kilnwick Percy Hall with its attractive lake, and Pocklington church tower. Pocklington, a lively market town of nearly 4,000 inhabitants, is 2½ miles to the west (and there is a bus, East Yorkshire and West Yorkshire 44, every two hours); here you may find accommodation at the *Station Hotel* (tel. Pocklington 3113), the *Feathers Hotel* (tel. 3155) and at the home of Mrs. M. O'Kelly, 15 Chapmangate, Pocklington (tel. 2687). William Wilberforce was a pupil at the grammar school in Pocklington. Pocklington church is a fine building, whose best feature is its majestic fifteenth century tower, with noble interior arches and amusing decorations. Since 1965 the railway has no longer served Pocklington, but there are frequent buses (East and West Yorkshire 46) for Beverley and Hull, York and Leeds, and also for Bridlington (no. 44) and a number of other destinations.

You have arrived via a gate at the B1246 road. Cross the road and go through an open gate, keeping to the left of the hedgerow to Wold Farm. (N.B. Be sure not to take the gravel track to Wold Farm further down the hill.) On your right are still long views of the Vale of York and also south-west towards Selby. Leave Wold Farm on your right and continue across the fields, at first next to a ploughed field, then on grass tracks. (Coming from the south, do not turn left down to Wold Farm; keep straight ahead, passing a piggery, to the road.) As you walk through the last field above Bratt Wood, move diagonally to your left to a gate (misleadingly marked Private Area on its far side) at the entrance to the wood, which is a beautiful sight in April and May, with primroses, bluebells and other spring flowers. (If you are going north, after leaving the gate bear to your left along the field; do not keep to the hedgerow on the right.) Carry on through Bratt Wood on the partly metalled road and come out on the Nunburnholme-Pocklington road at the sign marked "Bridle Road to Milling-ton". Turn to the left down the road for about 200 yards and enter a meadow on your right by the first (not the second) gate. After about 50 yards turn left through another gate and continue to a point opposite Nunburnholme church, where you gain the road by a third gate.

Nunburnholme village, which takes its name from the site of a long-vanished Benedictine priory, has no other hospitality than the village shop-cum-post office. (On Saturdays there are three buses, East Yorkshire 99, to Pocklington.) Its special attractions are the church and the old rectory. The church has a disappointing tower, but there is a beautifully decorated Norman window and a blocked Norman door in the north wall. Inside, the chief attractions are the richly carved Norman tower arch, full of zigzag ornamentation and fantastic faces, and the even more remarkable shaft formerly in the church-yard, now under the tower. This was once part of a cross; standing well over four feet high it is reputed to be either Saxon or Viking in origin and to date from the tenth or eleventh centuries. The repaired shaft has carvings of both people and animals, including the Mother and Child, dragons, a lamb and a centaur. Alan Binns suggests that the cross may be the work of "a very assimilated Viking", and terms it a "well-digested amalgam of Scandinavian and English styles." (*The Viking Century in East Yorkshire,* EYLHS 15, 1963)

Nunburnholme old rectory is a lovely, cream-painted Georgian building. It was the home of the ornithologist Francis Orpen Morris. who was rector of Nunburnholme from 1854 until his death at the age of 83 in 1893. Morris, who is buried next to his wife underneath the south wall of the church, was a prolific writer. His letters to *The Times* alone, we are told, would have filled a small volume. Among his many works were six volumes of *A History of British Birds* (1851-57), three volumes of *A Natural History of the Nests and Eggs of British Birds* (1853-56), four more on *A Natural History of British Moths* (1859-70) and five on *The County Seats of the Noblemen and Gentlemen of Great Britain and Ireland* (1866-80). His son, the Rev. M. C. F. Morris, who died in 1935, was also rector of Nunburnholme and a well-known writer on local subjects. One of his major works was a fascinating volume called *Yorkshire Folk-Talk* (1892), and his chapter on "The Wolds" in a volume somewhat misleadingly entitled *The British Workman* (1928), remains an excellent, knowledgeable introduction to the subject.

The younger Morris wrote of his father in a memorial volume of 1897 that he was "the staunchest of Tories", opposed to such novel doctrines as free schools ("The parents saved far more than the small weekly fee of a penny or twopence in children's clothing and in doctors' bills through their being kept for six hours of the day in a dry and warm school'.') and evolution ("Where is the setting forth of the doctrine of evolution in the Book of Genesis? I see no trace or sign of it".) The march of history has left Morris and many of his beliefs behind, but in their day both he and his son were among the most remarkable of country clergymen, and the elder Morris was influential in securing early legislation for the protection of birds.

From Nunburnholme village, turn off the road just south of the public telephone, go through a gate and cross a grassy field. Cross Nunburnholme Beck on a shaky plank bridge and ascend the hill on a grass track interspersed with crushed bricks, keeping the hedgerow on your left. At the gateposts turn sharply to the right, keeping the fence on your right. Note the good views behind and to the right, including the tower of Pocklington church. Keep next to the fence, and at the end of the field go through the gate at the corner and carry on across the next field, a pleasant meadow. Keep Thorns Wood immediately on your right, and leave the meadow through a gate. The route now becomes a green track which you follow to Partridge Hall Farm, the extensive view including Holme on Spalding Moor church on its little hill. Bear left at the farm, keeping the main buildings to your right. Then move right to the little beck, which you cross on a plank bridge, and continue to the road by a rickety stile. You come onto the road opposite the signpost marked "Londesborough 1", and it is this fairly busy road which you now follow. The site of the lost village of Cleaving and the woodland of Cleaving Plantation are on your right. Splendid views now open out as you

Nunburnholme village and Bratt Wood from the south, looking towards Pocklington.

approach Londesborough, to Shiptonthorpe and Market Weighton on the York-Hull road (A 1079), and beyond to the Humber and Lincolnshire, as well as Drax power station to the south-west. At Shiptonthorpe accommodation is offered by Mrs. G. Tennant, at "Edenhall," Holme Road, Shiptonthorpe, York, (tel. Holme on Spalding Moor 518).

At Londesborough there is again no more than a village shop to welcome the traveller, the penalty of being an estate village. However, it is very pretty, with numerous old houses with tiled roofs. Opposite the church is a stone house with a plaque giving its date as 1750, and to the right are two brick cottages of similar date. A little further on is an ancient barn of brick and stone with a slate roof. The church is interesting; the south porch has a rather crudely carved Norman doorway, with an ancient sundial and a Saxon cross above it. The outer porch wall has a number of old inscriptions, including one dated 1735, and two more sundials, one of them dated 1764. There is a fine churchyard, with a stone and cobble walk and two magnificent yews.

From the church make your way north-east to the entrance to Londesborough Park. Though but a shadow of its earlier self, the Park is delightful, consisting of 400 acres of woodland and pasture. Londesborough has an interesting history and many legends are attached to it. It is supposed to be the site of the lost Delgovitia, a Roman settlement, and in fact a portion of Roman road was found at the bottom of the lake in about 1895. It was also supposed to be the site of the summer palace of the kings of Northumbria and the place where the Saxon king Edwin was converted to Christianity in the year 626. What is true is that Londesborough has belonged to a number of families, including the Cliffords and Richard Boyle, third Earl of Burlington (1695-1753), who built Burlington House in London. It was Burlington who laid out Londesborough Park with lakes, terraces and waterfalls, and an avenue of elms in honour of the actor David Garrick. The Hall later fell to the Dukes of Devonshire, and the sixth Duke pulled the Hall down in 1819. The Duke was reported to have burst into tears when he revisited the site and saw the ruin he had caused, but he consoled himself by selling the 12,000 acres of Londesborough to George Hudson, the "railway king," in 1845, for £470,000. Hudson was busy planning the York-Market Weighton railway at the time (it opened in 1847), and he had a private station with a two-mile carriageway built through an avenue of trees to the house. Part of the avenue may still be seen, but the station buildings are now gone. After Hudson's financial collapse in 1849 the house was sold to Albert Denison, who was created first Baron Londesborough in 1850. (The family's wealth was created by commerce and banking; the barony was raised to an earldom in 1887.) When a census of landowners was carried out in 1873 the second Lord Londesborough was the second largest landowner in the East Riding (Sir Tatton Sykes of Sledmere owning slightly more), his 33,006 acres bringing in a rental of nearly £40,000 per annum. The Londesboroughs lived lavishly, entertaining royalty and being great racing figures, but as a result land had to be sold almost continuously from the end of the century. In 1937 the earldom died with the fourth Earl. The present owners of Londesborough Park are good friends to ramblers, but please co-operate by keeping to the public rights of way and not straying onto the private grounds.

The entrance to Londesborough Park bears a footpath sign reading "Market Weighton $2\frac{1}{4}$". Go down the stony track and continue past the sign marked Public Footpath, noticing the gate piers of the eighteenth century Hall. A hundred yards later there are two possibilities. If you go straight ahead, skirting the lake which you keep to your left, you will continue on the public right of way to Market Weighton. It is sign-posted, but ploughed up and obstructed for the last mile. At Market Weighton you can find dinner, bed and breakfast at the *Griffin* (tel. Market Weighton 3284) or the *Londesborough Arms* (tel. Market Weighton 2219), shops, and buses to Leeds, York, Beverley and Hull (East and West Yorkshire service 46) at two-hourly intervals. Market Weighton, a town of 2,000 inhabitants, is equidistant from York and Hull, about 19 miles from each, and is at the junction of five roads. It is thus much too traffic-ridden for most tastes. The spacious church has a tower with a top storey of brick, and there is a prominent Methodist church with Corinthian pilasters and round arches. From Market Weighton, if you wish to cheat a little, you can catch the 46 bus east to Arras Cottages and meet the Wolds Way five miles after you left it.

**Londesborough Park, with the Hall in the distance.
(Ramblers' Association).**

If you are determined to plod on, turn down the track which intersects from the left in Londesborough Park. The track forks after a hundred yards and here you turn right, past some old sheds. Note the excellent views back to Londesborough Hall. Cross the east end of the lake on the remains of a plank bridge, then go through the gate and across the meadowland of Londesborough Park. Go up the hill on the grass track, which gives continued good views back to the Hall. Leaving the Park through a gate, turn to the right, on a metalled road. After about a quarter of a mile the road turns to the right. Here a grass track goes straight on to the A 163 road. Follow this track, on the line of the old Roman road from Malton to Brough, to Towthorpe Corner, a busy spot where a County Council picnic site is being planned (very occasional buses to Driffield and Goole, East Yorkshire 11). Cross the improved road, continue past the remains of the old road and onto the track leading to Goodmanham, which leaves the old road to the left. At the hedgerow nearly half a mile on, turn sharply to the left. The track descends to the brick bridge of the former Selby-Market Weighton-Driffield railway (closed 1965), then climbs a hill to Goodmanham (keep left at the fork).

You come out opposite the church which forms the central feature of Goodmanham. It is a pretty village, with attractive old houses, especially the imposing Hall Garth, built of yellow brick with a fine portico. One of the houses near the church has a firemark on its side. The church is low and long; it is believed to stand on the site of a pagan temple destroyed in 626. According to the Venerable Bede, after the Saxon king Edwin was converted in 626 the High Priest Coifi himself led the destruction of the pagan temple. "This place", according to Bede, "where idols were, is still shewn, not far from York to the eastward beyond the River Derwent, and is now called Godmundingham, where the priest, by the inspiration of the true God, profaned the altars which he himself had consecrated." After that dramatic report, it is a comedown to have to report that the tower of Goodmanham church is disappointingly squat, but there is a fine Norman south doorway, a charmingly crooked Norman chancel arch and two remarkable fonts, one of them possibly Saxon, the other Tudor.

Goodmanham is a most satisfying village, but to most long-distance walkers its happiest feature will be the *Goodmanham Arms* (tel. Market Weighton 2379), the first public house on the Wolds Way since leaving Thixendale some fifteen miles earlier. Here you can expect a warming fire, drink, snacks and, if you enquire beforehand of Mrs. Swann, possibly dinner, bed and breakfast and cups of tea for rambling parties. Turn left past the church and continue to the east end of Goodmanham village. Here turn right onto the metalled road leading towards Etton, passing the sign for the Paxwold Girls' Guide camp. The road is pretty, the Wolds gradually getting steeper and affording nicely wooded views. On your left, just before you reach the now destroyed bridge of the former York-Beverley railway (closed 1965), is the Rifle Butts Quarry Geological Reserve, the property of the Yorkshire Naturalists' Trust. In the reserve 70 species of flowers are to be seen during the year, and the hillside has a rock exposure, showing Lower Lias, red and white chalk in a succession seen nowhere else in England. It is a pleasant place for a quiet stop. And while you are here you may want to know that a couple of miles to the north-east, at the former Kiplingcotes Station, is an attractive antique shop called Granny's Attic, and close to it the beginning of the Kiplingcotes Race Course. The Kiplingcotes race, about four miles long, is run annually on the third Thursday in March, and is reputed to be the oldest horse race in England, going back at least to the mid-sixteenth century.

Passing under the former railway bridge you come to a road junction, signposted to Market Weighton to the right, South Dalton and Etton to the left. Here you go straight ahead, through a gate and uphill on a grassy track. Behind you is a pleasant wooded Wold scene. Ahead, after you ascend the grassy hillside and go through another gate, is a long footslog of nearly two miles before reaching Arras Farm. The views are wide but not especially attractive, though there is a nice view of Goodmanham Dale on the left. Walk steadily uphill along the field edges on a definitive right of way to Arras, between the buildings of the farm community and out on the farm avenue to the York-Hull road (A 1079). From here there is a frequent bus service (East and West Yorkshire 46) throughout the day to points between Hull, Beverley, York and Leeds. An AA telephone box is on your right, a public call box on your left. (Coming from the south, be sure to take the farm road to the left, not the road called Kiplingcotes Lane to the right.) Arras is a sizeable settlement, and as mentioned earlier, it had a large graveyard of the Iron Age Parisi tribe.

CROSSING the main York-Hull road, walk down the metalled road opposite. Although it leads to Sancton, it is without a signpost and carries little traffic. Follow the road for about a mile, leaving it where it turns sharply to the right not long after Hessleskew Farm. A grass track leads straight ahead, between a ploughed field and a hedgerow, a large horse-chestnut tree in the field acting as a good signpost. Shortly before the turn a circle of trees, about 300 yards to the left, surrounds a deep pit 200 yards round. The area around the pit, the supposed site of a Roman arena, has yielded a number of archaeological remains, as mentioned in chapter 1.

At the end of the field at Gare Gate the track turns sharply to the right; do not follow it straight ahead to the Newbald-Etton road. A Public Footpath signpost indicates the direction which you are to follow. Keep to the edge of a grassy field and descend the hill; in about quarter of a mile you reach the little wood called Hessleskew Gare. Where the wood begins the route has been ploughed out and you must follow the field edge. Cross the fence at the end of the ploughed field and follow the field of long grass down the valley, with a line of trees on your right, the line soon becoming a copse ascending the hill. Continue along the valley, below bare hills prettily fringed with a line of trees. The path, though faint, is discernible through the grass. The pretty valleys form a characteristic Wold scene, typical of much of the country through which you have walked since leaving Filey.

Cross the fence and keep to the left of the hedge along the bottom of the hill. Walk through the long grass to Syke House Farm (Newbald Sike). Just before reaching the farm buildings turn sharply left through the gate, being sure not to follow the farm track further round to the left and down the valley, where it leads to a chalk pit. Having gone through the gate, continue up the hill on grassland. About a mile north-west of Syke House is the village of Sancton. It possesses a striking monument in the octagonal lantern tower of its church, one of the finest and

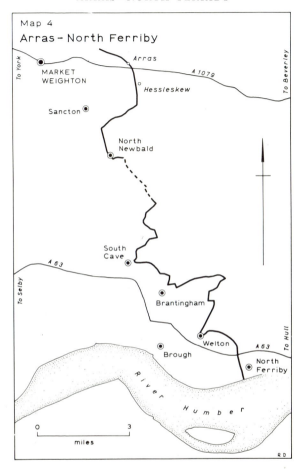

Map 4
Arras - North Ferriby

most unusual towers in the East Riding. At the age of 85, John Wesley preached here in 1788. Sancton also has a public house, the *Star Inn,* which does not offer accommodation. One bus a day (East Yorkshire 5X, not Sundays) goes to Hull, one to Market Weighton and Pocklington. The archaeology of the Sancton area has already been touched on (chapter 1).

At the top of the hill you reach another gate; go through it and along a hedgerow. Cross a stile which gives onto a large

57

ploughed field (definitive right of way again). Keep to the right-hand edge of this field and the next one, until you reach the remains of a track and begin to descend. There are lovely views down towards North Newbald and the hills beyond. Go through an open gate and so towards Newbald on a cart road. (Coming from the south be sure to go between the concrete posts and the open gate to the left; do not follow the farm road round to the right and Dot Hill Farm.) Reaching another gate at the bottom of the hill, turn left onto the metalled road and continue past new houses to the junction of Beverley Road and Eastgate. The centre of North Newbald village is a short distance to the west. (From the south turn left at the Beverley Road-Eastgate junction down Townside, following the road to the left but being careful not to turn sharply onto Spring Bank. The turn up the hill is at the second gate along the metalled road after the houses end, and is signposted Public Footpath—or was—the sign had disappeared the last time I was there.)

North Newbald is a pretty village and contains some attractive Georgian houses. Its principal buildings are grouped round one of the most charming village greens in the East Riding. Two handsome public houses, the *Gnu Inn* and the *Tiger Inn,* close the view at the south-west corner of the green. See the fine notice inside the *Tiger Inn* announcing an auction in North Newbald in 1851. Neither pub offers accommodation, but two addresses for bed and breakfast are: Mrs. D. Grainger, West-field House, North Newbald (tel. North Newbald 219) and Mr. and Mrs. L. Cross, Ings House, South Newbald Road, North Newbald (tel. North Newbald 685). One bus a day (East Yorkshire 5X, not Sundays) goes to Hull, one to Market Weighton and Pocklington. Not far beyond the pubs is a fish and chip shop (with somewhat irregular hours), and before you reach that important institution is Newbald church, a largely Norman building. The church has four splendid Norman doorways, rich with carvings, an aisleless Norman nave, fine tower arches and a somewhat squat thirteenth century tower with good pinnacles. There are (according to the vicar) no fewer than fourteen Norman windows in the church, many of them enriched with zigzag and other decoration. A thirteenth century font rests on eight clustered piers and is covered with a lovely leaf design. One of the most interesting memorial tablets commemorates Sir Philip Monckton, a supporter of the king during the Civil War, who had three horses shot from under him at "Naseby Field" and was elected M.P. for Scarborough in 1670. Outside the church, pilgrims' crosses may be seen on the south door and there are numerous masons' marks. Altogether, North Newbald is rivalled only by Wintringham as the finest church on the Wolds Way.

For the next two miles the route of the Wolds Way is not yet fixed. The intention is to leave the village by Burgate, the road leading to Little Weighton. About half a mile beyond the village opposite a hedgerow, a gate on the right gives onto a track leading into the lovely valley known as Cowdale. From the meadow there are fine views on all sides, and the mile through the charming Forestry Commission Deep Dale plantation is quiet and peaceful. (A Forestry Commission notice at the north entrance of the plantation asking you to shut the gate gives some hope that public access will be granted.) The views back to Deep Dale from the south are also very fine. However, it has not yet been possible to agree the route through Deep Dale, though it is to be hoped that this will be done in the near future. Moreover, after the route crosses the South Newbald-Walkington road, a narrow, metalled strip know as Whin Lane, there is an arable field about 250 yards wide before you reach the B 1230, the Beverley-North Cave road (no buses). No right of way is claimed to exist across this field, and the farmer is not unnaturally unwilling to concede one until adequate compensation and a footpath creation order have been carried out. (A possible route for a creation order is a narrow strip between two fields.) Thus the only possible route at present is to follow the Little Weighton road from North Newbald until it reaches the B 1230, then turning right on this busy road until, after about a mile, it reaches a white gate on the left from which a farm road leads to the now vanished High Drewton Farm.

Turn down the farm road, which gives fine views of the shining Humber and north Lincolnshire, views which will be with you now for much of the rest of the Way. When you reach the site of High Drewton Farm turn to the left, then sharply to the right on the track after leaving the site. (Coming from the south be sure to turn left past the farm site at this point; do not continue straight ahead on the track.) After about fifty yards another track joins yours at a right angle. Follow the latter track down the hill, with the fine views of the Humber and north Lincolnshire continuously before you. The track descends between fields of standing corn, then runs past the eastern edge of Austin's Dale. This is a lovely dale, with mature trees and young plantations; between the fringe of trees on your right can be seen the massive, white St. Austin's Stone. St. Augustine is said to have preached here when he

Comber Dale (Ramblers' Association).

visited England just before 600 A.D. The stone, which is in its
natural setting, is a prominent landmark from the track.

As you walk downhill, more trees spread round you until
you are walking through a pretty arbour. At its end you pass
through a white gate and along the track to the farm known as
Drewton Cottage. The track goes round two sides of the farm,
leaving it on your right, then continuing downhill and becoming an earth road. You now descend into another little
wood and turn right, leaving to your left the pretty waters
where Drewton Beck breaks into a pool. Shortly after leaving
the Beck and ascending a little hill, you turn left off the road
onto a cart track. Pass through a white gate and cross the old
Hull and Barnsley railway line on a bridge with brick walls.
You are still on a clear track, as you have been ever since High
Drewton Farm. Walk parallel to the old railway line, ascending
and then descending a hill, following the track round to the
right. Now a green lane, the track reaches a white gate and
becomes a path, following the left edge of a field of corn. On
the left is another attractive wood.

60

The Hull-Barnsley railway was one of the last railways built in the East Riding. A number of unsuccessful attempts were made to build a line connecting the two towns, a matter of increasing urgency to Hull, which felt that the North-Eastern Railway was systematically ignoring it in favour of ports in the north-east. K. A. MacMahon writes in his *The Beginnings of the East Yorkshire Railways* (EYLHS 3, 1953), that when the Bill for the line finally gained royal assent in 1879 there was a parade in Hull. "The Kirkella Harmonic Brass Band led a motley collection of Conservatives, Liberals, Secularists, Radicals and the Magna Charta Association, while the Cottingham Harmonic Brass Band lent its aid by leading a contingent which included the Burns Club sandwiched between the Romans Friendly Society and representatives of the Royal Antediluvian Order of Buffaloes." In January, 1880, the first sod was cut in Hull, and a choir of 2,000 voices sang a specially composed "Song of the Men of Hull", which began:

> *Once more the shout for we are free,*
> *By no monopoly confined.*
> *To work our town's high destiny,*
> *The lot by Providence designed.*

But throughout the years that followed, the H & B found great difficulty in making ends meet. Finally, in 1955 all passenger services were ended (having been curtailed in 1932), while freight traffic stopped in 1959. Perhaps British Rail does not ignore Hull as the North-Eastern Railway did, but the passing of an attractive and well-loved line was a sad event.

At the end of the wood, cross the fence at the remains of a stile. The path joins a second and clearer path, and here you turn to the right and uphill. (To the left and below are the waters of Weedley Springs and the old railway line; coming from the south turn left by the edge of the wood just before the descent to Weedley Springs and the old line, easily identified by the cutting through which it runs.) You now ascend Comber Dale. The hills and woods make a superb scene, and although this is a popular spot there are seldom large numbers of visitors at any one time. Only the ugly electricity pylons create a jarring note. At the top of the hill you reach the unmade county road called Swinescaif Road, from which there are again fine views of the Humber. (Coming from the south turn left just to the right of the sign marked Private Property, cross the remaining bit of the gate and go down the path keeping just to the right of the hedgerow.) At Swinescaif Road turn right and continue to the west for about quarter of a mile. There are very pretty views of the valley and the wooded hills opposite, and, closer at hand, masses of brambles in late summer. (Brambles are also found along the woods to the south.) Writing of a spot very close to where you are now, A. J. Brown commented: "Walking thus in the early morning with the sun sparkling on the dew, the air laden with scents and the golden Wolds beyond, a man may thank his lucky stars that he is walking the Wolds Way, whatever the day may bring."

A few yards past the eastern edge of Little Wold Plantation (and close to its western edge also) is a broad track leading through the lovely wood under an arbour of branches. Continue down this track; near the southern edge of the wood is a bench affording nice views of the eastern edge of South Cave and the hills. (Shortly before the bench another track turns off through the wood; coming from the south be sure to keep to the track to the right and not to follow the other one.) The track becomes an unmade county road and descends the hill through pleasant scenes towards South Cave. Before long the road becomes metalled; from the south be sure to keep straight ahead at this point and not follow the metalled road round to the left where it is signposted Private Drive. You are now on Little Wold Lane, which leads out onto the Beverley Road and the eastern edge of South Cave.

The centre of South Cave is less than quarter of a mile to the west. There are two public houses, both of them providing bed and breakfast. These are the *Bear* (tel. North Cave 2461) and the *Fox and Coney* (tel. North Cave 2275), which dates from 1739. (This guide is strictly impartial, but it is perhaps worth pointing out that when A. J. Brown was walking his Wolds Way forty years ago he found the *Fox and Coney* "a very hospitable old road-house which I can thoroughly recommend.") There is also accommodation at *Cave Castle Hotel* (tel. North Cave 2345), half a mile west of the centre of South Cave and next to the parish church, standing in its own grounds This rebuilt "castle", on the site of an earlier great house, will be a bit on the pricey side for many walkers. The church has little of interest, though it has a handsome fifteenth century tower with Perpendicular windows. South Cave is a largish, straggling village with a number of shops. There is also a yellow brick town hall, built in 1796 and standing prominently in the centre of the village. A clock commemorates the Jubilee of 1887, and hanging from the roof of the open ground floor are meat hooks which were used when markets were held at this spot. There are frequent buses (East Yorkshire 3, 4, 5) to Hull, and also (not so frequent) to Goole and Selby.

Returning to the Wolds Way, from the end of Little Wold Lane turn right onto the Beverley Road and left just before the bungalow a few yards on. The route goes through a farm, turning left at its end and then diagonally to the east between cornfields on a clear track. You then ascend a hill, from which there are nice views behind towards South Cave, the Humber and the hills. At the top of the hill you join an unmade farm road which leads to the right to Mount Airy Farm. When you reach Mount Airy, be sure to turn to the right (as waymarked) and go through the farm yard; do not continue straight past the farm on the unmade road. It is about half a mile to Wood-ale (or Warrenhouse) Farm, along the edge of a wood and then descending into Woodale. From Mount Airy the Ramblers' Association has cleared the path which runs along the edge of the wood, and waymarked it with yellow arrows, the only such waymarking (at the time of writing) on the Wolds Way. As you walk along the wood edge, with the fence on your right, notice how suddenly and sharply the land falls away on your left. At the end of the wood you cross a fence and follow the waymarked route down the hill to Woodale. Despite the obtrusive electricity pylons, there are splendid views down the hills and to the Humber.

As you reach Woodale Farm you will notice more waymarks. There is no need to go through the farmyard; turn to the left, following the yellow arrows through a gate and then again left, steeply uphill along the track. (Coming from the south, turn to the right as waymarked just before reaching the farmyard.) As you ascend, note the views back to the shining Humber. Reaching the wood you will see a stile in a corner, some thirty yards from the gate on its left edge. The route is for the last time waymarked; cross over the stile and follow the clearly defined path steeply downhill between the trees. In contrast to the bare hills which have hitherto characterised much of the Wolds Way, the route now passes through sizeable tracts of woodland, and this stretch through Waltham's Wold Plantation and down to the Brantingham-Riplingham road is among the prettiest sections.

You reach the road by the gate. (Coming from the south the gate is in front of a sign somewhat misleadingly marked Brantingham Estate Private; while the estate is private property the path itself is a definitive public right of way.) You are now in the beautiful, wooded Brantingham Dale, the most popular

63

valley within easy reach of Hull (about ten miles to the east). Quarter of a mile to your left is a popular open space (please don't add to the litter already there), but the Wolds Way route is to the right, down the lovely valley road to Brantingham church, a little less than half a mile away. The church is picturesquely sited; the aisleless building has a good tower and a nicely moulded south door, but its best feature is without doubt its splendid location, surrounded by wooded hills. (Note the photograph inside the porch, showing Brantingham church and Dale in snow.) Next to the church is a house selling minerals, ices and teas, a popular spot. Despite numerous visitors the area around the church is never anything but charming. Brantingham village, another half mile to the south-west, has attractive houses and a pretty village pond. The public house, the *Triton* (closed on Sundays), does not offer accommodation, but the buses serving South Cave also stop at Brantingham, continuing to Hull, and to Goole and Selby.

The Wolds Way goes uphill through the attractive Wandhills Plantation from Brantingham Church. Just to the left of the churchyard, enter the woods on the clear path and then go straight uphill on a wide track, a steep climb (Where the tracks diverge, keep to the right fork). Reaching the top of the hill, turn right just before a gate, walk through the top edge of the woodland and so, after about quarter of a mile, out to the metalled road at the point called Spout Hill. To your right the road leads steeply down to Brantingham village; if you descend, there is a lovely view across the grass to Brantingham church. Instead of going down to Brantingham, however, turn to the left. From the top of the hill there are wide views of the Humber, north Lincolnshire and, on clear days, as far as York Minster. For a little less than quarter of a mile the road is metalled. After passing the entrance to Brantingham Wold Farm the road becomes a wide green lane, a pretty route with woods on the right and arable fields on the left.

Continue on this charming lane for over half a mile, until it joins the Elloughton-Riplingham road. This road, which is metalled, bears round to the left. Follow it for about quarter of a mile to the point at which it meets the fairly busy Welton-Riplingham road. At this point you join an earth track immediately opposite. The track passes through a slender woodland, then, narrowing, continues between ploughed fields with a row of trees on the right, descending gradually. This is pleasant valley country, rich and lush. Somewhat over half a mile from the road the path turns sharply right, to the south-west. It is important to make this turn, which is at a

A litter-cleaning party passes Brantingham church. (Roger Cooper)

very acute angle, and not to continue on to Wauldby Scrogs and Raywell, as I did on one occasion. Where the route turns there are two white gates at right angles. Go through both, following the track which is still apparent on the ground, though faint. It continues to the west of the round wood known as Fox Covert and through pleasant meadows and between fields to Wauldby Manor Farm.

Clearer now, the track passes the farm cottages which are on your right and reaches the farm road at the waters of Wauldby Dam. Wauldby is the site of another deserted village. Here turn right, keeping to the left of the two forks, with the farm buildings on your right and Wauldby Manor with its disused chapel on your left. The manor and chapel (which dates from the nineteenth century) are a pretty sight through the trees. Continue past the farm on the gravel road out to the Welton-Riplingham road. Notice the Humber and the Wolds of north Lincolnshire, and closer at hand the newly-erected 600-foot chimney of the Capper Pass refinery, part of the Rio Tinto Zinc organisation. (Coming from the south, keep to the left on the road marked "All Tradesmen and Farm Vehicles", and be sure not to take the private road to Wauldby

Manor".) Continue along the metalled road for about 500 yards; a path runs next to the hedgerow, so there is no need to walk on the road itself. Just before reaching Dale Plantation you come to a white gate on your left. Go through it and down the hill, admiring the view back to Wauldby. The path runs between the plantation and the edge of a cultivated field. Near the bottom of the hill you enter the top of Welton Dale, crossing the fence and following the grassy path between trees.

The track through Welton Dale is the most bitterly contested footpath in the East Riding. It was included on the Draft and Provisional Maps of Rights of Way, but was one of the 1200 paths omitted from the Definitive Map due to the landowner's objection. It is now again on the Revised Draft Map of Rights of Way, but the struggle over the path has resulted in a colleague and myself being sued in the High Court. Welton Dale is one of the prettiest, most secluded and unspoilt valleys in the East Riding, and it is stoutly maintained by the Ramblers' Association and others that there is a right of way through it. The Association has also suggested that the area would be very suitable for use as a Country Park. But let the reader beware; the owner will only yield when and if the track is legally decided to be a right of way, and those who

66

Scenes at Welton. Opposite: The Green Dragon inn. Above: Two views of Welton Dale. (Author)

do not wish to join the defendants in the Battle of Welton Dale may well prefer to follow the road (with extensive views of the Humber) into Welton village.

The grassy path previously mentioned leads, after several hundred yards, to the left and the Dale bottom. Before turning left you pass just east of the interesting mausoleum of the Raikes family, a large circular structure 38 feet high erected by Robert Raikes in 1818, with a domed roof and well-proportioned classical trimmings. It has suffered from attacks by vandals but is now in reasonably good repair. Walking south through Welton Dale, Dale Plantation is on your right. On the left is a fence and beyond it the hill slopes, mostly bare, with some scrub and a few trees. The whole scene is one of great beauty. At the end of the Dale you pass the game-keeper's cottage and then, on your left, Welton Springs, a long and pretty pond with geese and ducks. There is also Welton High Mill, a five-storey brick and tile building, which was worked by water until 1946 and by electricity as late as 1966. The top two storeys were added in 1861, the lower ones look Georgian. (See K. J. Allison, *East Riding Water-Mills,* EYLHS 26, 1970). There are also attractive out-buildings.

You now continue into Welton on Dale Road, which is metalled from the mill. Welton is a very pretty village. There are several attractive eighteenth century houses, among them

Welton House, sheltered behind trees, and the stuccoed Creyke House in the middle of the village, with handsome square and round windows. Another fine house is Welton Manor, a yellow brick mansion of the early nineteenth century standing immediately opposite the public house, the *Green Dragon,* in extensive grounds. The *Green Dragon* (no accommodation) is an attractive pub, and is reputed to be the place where Dick Turpin, the highwayman, was arrested in 1739 and carried off to York Assizes. Turpin still arouses strong feelings, for a Welton resident described him to me as a "boozy old reprobate"; a facsimile of the York assize record of his trial may be seen inside the *Green Dragon.'* This indicates that Turpin was arrested for stealing horses in the parish of Welton. Welton has also a village green, a stream and a pond on which ducks swim. Opposite the church is a distinctive Victorian red brick building with yellow trimmings, which began life as a chapel, became a grocers-cum-drapers and is now disused.

Welton Church is unattractive, its tower squat and ugly. Too much restoration has left a church of little beauty, but there are some interesting memorials, including a stone effigy of a knight in armour with crossed legs just inside the south door. Outside the north-east end of the church is a remarkable gravestone. This is the grave of Jeremiah Simpson, a copy made in 1863 of an earlier stone, now at the foot of the grave. The epitaph (the copy has been attractively done in authentic facsimile) reads as follows:

Here lieth He ould
Ieremy who hath
eight times maried
been but now in his
ould age he lies
in his cage under
The gras so green
which Ieremiah Simp
son departed this
Life in the 84 yeare
of his age in the
year of our Lord
1719

The South Cave-Brantingham buses also stop at Welton.

Leave Welton by Chapel Hill Road, south-east of Dale Road. Chapel Hill Road is a quiet country lane with pretty views to the left into Welton Dale and wide views of the broad and curving Humber. After a little over quarter of a mile an unmade road comes in from the right. This is the road running south of the Portland Cement quarry; on the left a red sign marked DANGER indicates the limit of the quarry. At this point a track leads to the right, to the southern edge of Bow Plantation. The route continues immediately south of the plantation, with an arable field on your right. The giant chimney and works of Capper Pass are between you and the Humber, but despite this ugliness the views are extensive and grand. The route is difficult to follow, but gradually it becomes distinct, first as a path, then a green lane and finally a cart track, part of what was once a carriage drive through trees from Welton to the Humber. The track is worth following, since the alternative, the road past the cement quarry, has a view even more depressing than the fairly distant sight of Capper Pass. About 400 yards west of the Melton-Swanland road the cart track leads left to the road past the cement works, and as the route ahead is blocked it is necessary to continue out of the quarry by this road.

Crossing the Melton-Swanland road (Melton Bottom), go through a white gate slightly to the right and uphill into the woods of Terrace Plantation. From this point you will be among trees until the end of the Wolds Way. The track passes

Church features. Left: The south door of North Newbald church. Right: The tomb of Jeremiah Simpson at Welton. (Geoff Mell)

69

End of the Wolds Way. The author at North Ferriby foreshore.

a scouts' camping site, then narrows and becomes a footpath, which you follow, crossing a cart track, to the south. (Coming from the south go almost straight across the track and follow the path into the wood.) The path continues through the trees, widening and then again narrowing, and reaches the main A 63 Hull-Leeds road. Cross the road with care and turn right. A few yards later you come to a gate on the left, which gives onto a track through Long Plantation. The track crosses over the main railway line from Hull to the west, skirts new houses on the edge of North Ferriby, and, passing through a gate, reaches the Humber foreshore, 67 miles from the starting point at Filey Brigg. The Humber is two miles wide at this point, and it is a good spot to stop and ponder for a time on the varied route which you have walked. Hull is eight miles to the east; Hessle, where the Humber Bridge is to be built, a little over three miles. (The bridge forms a link in what may eventually become the Viking Way, a walk from Saltburn, on the north Yorkshire coast, to the border of Suffolk. The coastal length of the Cleveland Way and the Wolds Way form a substantial part of the route, and sections in Lincolnshire and most of the Norfolk coast are already public rights of way.) On the Lincolnshire side of the river you can see (from left to right), the chimneys of Barton-on-Humber, the Wolds, South Ferriby (in trees) and its attendant cement works. On North Ferriby foreshore near where you are standing there was excavated in 1946 Europe's oldest known plank-built boat, 50 feet long and dating from 1200 B.C.; a model can be seen in Hull Museum.

To your left is a path on the bank, skirting the edge of the gardens of new houses. It leads to Humber Road, and so to Ferriby railway station, the first working station you have met since leaving Filey. North Ferriby is a sizeable village, now heavily populated with Hull commuters, and has numerous shops. The buses stop at the public house called the *Duke of Cumberland* (no accommodation) and, while they take longer than the train, unlike the latter they stop at Ferriby on Sunday. Both bus (East Yorkshire 3, 4, 5) and train go to Hull and to Goole, Selby and other points west. It is perhaps best to find accommodation in one of these larger places (In Hull, Mrs. M. Jackson, 788 Holderness Road, no telephone, caters especially for Wolds Way walkers.), but the Ferriby Hall Club (tel. Hull 643472) provides bed and breakfast on Monday to Friday; so too (also on weekends) does the *Hull Crest Motel* (tel. Hull 631122), on the main A 63 road outside Ferriby. North Ferriby church has been rebuilt (a pretty print inside dates from the time of the rebuilding in 1846) and only a few inscriptions are of much interest. Chief among these is a memorial in the form of an obelisk to the Etherington family of Hull and Ferriby (1819). In a nicely lettered script it embroiders on a contemporary theme, the words of which may be of some interest to those with sore feet:

> *Taught of God, we should view losses, sickness*
> *Pain and Death, but as the several trying*
> > *stages by which a*
> *Good Man, like Joseph, is conducted from a*
> > *Tent to a Court.*
> *Sin his Disorder, Christ his Physician,*
> *Pain his Medecine, the Bible his*
> > *Support, the Grave his Rest*
> *And Death itself an Angel expressly sent to*
> *Release the worn out labourer*
> *Or Crown the faithfull Soldier.*

With this quotation and a final salute to the Wolds Way, this guide may fittingly end.

71

Ramblers on the High Wolds. (Ramblers' Association)